Revelation and Sacred Scripture

Scripture

A Primary Source Reader

Timothy Milinovich

saint mary's press

The publishing team included Gloria Shahin, editorial director; Steven McGlaun, development editor; prepress and manufacturing coordinated by the production departments of Saint Mary's Press.

Cover Image @ The Crosiers / Gene Plaisted, OSC

Printed in the United States of America

1358

ISBN 978-1-59982-127-6, print
ISBN 978-1-59982-467-3, Kno
ISBN 978-1-59982-233-4, Saint Mary's Press Online Learning Environment

Contents

Introduction

As you have come to learn with your family and friends, communication is the most important part of a relationship. A relationship in which the parties do not talk, write, or express their feelings to one another is a relationship that cannot last.

Our relationship with God is no different. We require communication with God to make the relationship work. On our part, we express our love to God through prayer, worship, stewardship of creation, and love of neighbor. For his part, God communicates to us through Revelation—meaning, God reveals himself to us to initiate and foster our covenant relationship.

The fact that God reveals himself to us tells us two things: (1) God loves us enough to communicate with us and maintain this relationship with his creation, and (2) God knows we can recognize and understand his love and his will that he reveals to us in both infinite and finite ways.

Although broken at times, we remain God's beloved children, created in his glorious image—it is this initial loving connection of Creator and creation that marks humanity as unique among the rest of the created world. We can understand God's revealed will and can return with responses of loving worship of our own—it is a love story, a relationship, like no other in the world.

God reveals himself in a variety ways; through the beauty and order of natural creation and life, in the Holy Scriptures, in the Tradition of the Church, and in the person of Jesus Christ.

This is our faith: that Jesus Christ, "God with us," remains with us in the Church through the Holy Spirit, demonstrated in the Sacraments, and the liturgy of the Mass—in which Christ, God's living Word, is proclaimed to be heard with the ear of our hearts and by which we take part in Christ's sacrifice for the new covenant.

This reader, *Revelation and Sacred Scripture*, serves as a companion for your study of Sacred Scripture. It contains readings from saints, popes, Church documents, and modern scholars that fall under five parts. The first part engages the issue of how we can know God. In the second part, we find readings that discuss the nature and importance of the Scriptures. The third part provides a variety of methods for interpreting the historical and spiritual levels of God's Word. An overview of the Scriptures and the innate relationship of the Old and New Testaments is found in the fourth part. Finally, the fifth part addresses the four Gospels.

The goal of this reader is to make relevant Catholic teaching about the Scriptures accessible to you. This reader is intended to empower you with the ability to study and understand God's Word in a way that will deepen your relationship with God and your love for his Church.

Part 1
How Do We Know about God?

1 Humanity Seeks God, and God Reveals His Plan in a Grand Drama

Introduction

Catechism means "teaching." For the Catholic Church, this term reflects the Apostolic **Tradition** that has been taught and handed down through the centuries. Throughout the Church's history, Church leaders have written many forms of minor catechisms. One of the earliest known is called the *Didache* (the Teaching of the Twelve Apostles), which dates to the late first or mid second century. Saint Augustine (AD 354–430), Saint John Chrysostom (ca. 347–407), and other major teachers in the early Church wrote their own catechisms to teach the message of salvation in an organized manner to a particular audience. These catechisms cited the Scriptures often and relied on an educationally effective structure to aid their audience in understanding the teachings.

During the Middle Ages, the quality and content of many minor catechisms declined. A minor catechism is a resource developed to help teach specific groups or regions, and is intended to be a summary of a major catechism. A major catechism is a resource developed to guide the creation of minor catechisms and is intended for use primarily by clergy, teachers, and catechists. The minor catechisms at

Tradition From the Latin, *tradere*, meaning "to hand on," referring to the process of passing on the Gospel message. Tradition, which began with the oral communication of the Gospel by the Apostles, was written down in the Scriptures, is handed down and lived out in the life of the Church, and is interpreted by the Magisterium under the guidance of the Holy Spirit.

this time often presented questions and direct answers that para-
phrased Tradition and rarely cited or quoted the Scriptures directly.
Martin Luther (1483–1506), a Roman Catholic monk who began
the Protestant Reformation, criticized this form of catechism. In
response the bishops at the Council of Trent decreed the development of a new major catechism to guide the development of sound
and accurate minor catechisms. The catechism developed by the
Council of Trent and published in 1566 consisted of four main
parts: creed, sacraments, morality, and spirituality.

In the mid 1980s, about twenty years after the close of Vatican Council II, a synod of bishops requested that a compendium
of Catholic doctrine be created. In 1986 Pope John Paul II (1920–
2005) called together a commission of bishops and cardinals for
this purpose. Three years later, in 1989, the commission sent the
text they had created to all the bishops worldwide for review and
consultation. The final draft of this document, which incorporated
the responses from the world's bishops, was submitted in 1991 to
Pope John Paul II for his official approval.

On June 25, 1992, the *Catechism of the Catholic Church
(CCC)*, a new major catechism, was officially approved by Pope
John Paul II. The *CCC* follows the same four-part structure as the
Trent catechism. Although it is one of the best-selling Catholic
books in America (second only to the Bible), this edition was origi-
nally intended primarily for bishops, priests, scholars, teachers,
catechists, and lay ministers of pastoral formation. This is why the
CCC is often difficult for a nontheologian to read.

The *CCC* was published with the understanding that national
conferences of bishops would publish adaptations to this official
Catechism that would teach faithfully the Apostolic Tradition in a
way that engaged particular local issues for each national audience. In the United States, the most recent adaptation, the *United
States Catholic Catechism for Adults* (also known as the *Adult
Catechism*), was published by the **United States Conference of
Catholic Bishops** in 2006. It was written to be accessible to a wide
audience and follows the same effective four-part structure used in

United States Conference of Catholic Bishops The organization that consists of all U.S. Catholic bishops, who address matters related to the Church on the national level. They also publish materials for Catholics in the United States.

the 1566 and 1992 catechisms. This catechism also includes stories about American saints and reflection questions relevant to Catholics living in the United States today.

The reading for this chapter addresses humanity's inner desire to seek God and ponder questions like "Why am I here?" "Why do bad things happen?" and "How should I live my life?" This excerpt from the *United States Catholic Catechism for Adults* teaches that these questions are answered by God's Revelation. God reveals himself in the beauty of creation. In a special way, God reveals his saving plan for humanity in the covenant with Abraham and the Israelites and through the words of his prophets and the Apostles. Thus, God's Revelation takes place within the drama of salvation history. The message of this salvation—found in the Scriptures, Tradition, and the teaching of the Magisterium—provides an ongoing Revelation through the Church for all those who continue to seek God today.

Excerpt from the *United States Catholic Catechism for Adults*

By the United States Conference of Catholic Bishops

Through the use of reason, we can learn much about God from both creation and conscience, but Revelation enables us to learn about God's inner life and his loving plan to save us from sin and share in his divine life. No amount of unaided thinking could penetrate such a mystery. God freely chose to share this hidden mystery with us. God's sharing was an act of friendship for us, revealing himself as one reveals his or her heart to a friend. Love does such things.

> " *Revelation is the self-disclosure of the living God.* "

God's Revelation unfolded gradually throughout history. "Wishing to open up the way to heavenly salvation, he manifested himself to our first parents from the very beginning. After the fall, he buoyed them up with the hope of salvation, by promising redemption" (Second Vatican Council, *Dogmatic Constitution on Divine Revelation* [*Dei Verbum;* DV], no. 3; cf. Gn 3:15).

God continued over the succeeding centuries to provide providential care for those he created in his image and likeness. He called Abraham to make of him a great nation, a chosen people through whom salvation would come to the world. In the encounter of God with Moses, God reveals himself as *"I AM WHO AM."* These words reveal something about God, who, nevertheless, still remains mysterious. God is revealed as the source of all that is, but who he is will be revealed still further as he continues his loving work for his people. The prophets, in reflecting on God's actions, will make clearer the nature of God. But the clearest Revelation will come in Jesus Christ.

"In times past, God spoke in partial and various ways to our ancestors; in these last days he spoke to us through a son" (Heb 1:1–2). This Son was Jesus Christ, the fullness of Revelation. Wonderful indeed is this mystery of our faith in Jesus Christ, as we say in professing it, "[He] was manifested in the flesh, / vindicated in the Spirit; / seen by angels; / proclaimed to the Gentiles, / believed throughout the world, / taken up in glory" (1 Tm 3:16).

Revelation is the self-disclosure of the living God. God shows himself by both great deeds, as narrated for us in Scripture, and by the words that illumine the meaning of these deeds (see DV, no. 2). In Revelation, the tremendous gulf between God and the human race is bridged. More profoundly God desires to have an intimate relationship with all people. The process of Revelation, which took centuries to unfold, reached its magnificent fulfillment in the life, death, and Resurrection of Jesus Christ.

Revelation is the act by which God speaks to and forms a covenant people.[1] The covenant between God and humanity was first established with Noah after the great Flood, when God in his mercy promised that never again would there be a catastrophe that threatens the existence of all of humanity. God entered into a covenant later with Abraham and then with the people of Israel at the time of their exodus from slavery in Egypt under the leadership of Moses. He affirmed that they will always be his people.

This is the grand drama of the dialogue between God and his people that takes place in the lived history of the people encompassed by his love. It includes the people's **inspired** interpretation of historical events that reflects an ever greater understanding of God's will and presence as they advanced on their pilgrimage through the centuries.

It requires faith to respond to God's revealing word and to perceive the divine action in history. There are those who do not have faith or who consciously reject living in faith. They cannot or will not perceive God's presence or action in the world and sometimes scoff at or ridicule those who do. But for many people, God makes faith possible and with the guidance of the Holy Spirit faith helps those people to grow in an appreciation of how God has worked in history to love and save us.

God's Revelation disturbed and changed the patriarchs, prophets, Apostles, and others. When Moses encountered God in the burning bush, Moses trembled and took off his shoes, for he stood on holy ground (cf. Ex 3:1–6). **Isaiah** beheld the glory of God, and when the vision disappeared he saw himself in a brand-new light, "Woe is me, I am doomed! For I am a man of unclean lips" (Is 6:5). Faced with the revelation of divine power in Jesus, Peter begged, "Depart from me, Lord, for I am a sinful man" (Lk 5:8). Revelation calls for a response of faith and conversion, not just in times past, but today as well.

Because the Christian covenant is definitive, there will be no new public Revelation until the final glorious manifestation of Jesus Christ at the end days (DV, no. 4). All that is needed for salvation has already been revealed. What are called *private revelations,* that is, messages such as those given by the Blessed Virgin Mary at Lourdes and

inspired Written by human beings with the guidance of the Holy Spirit to teach without error those truths necessary for our salvation.

Isaiah One of the most prominent prophets of the Old Testament. New Testament authors often cite him as one who prophesied Christ's Incarnation and Crucifixion.

Fatima, add nothing to what was publicly revealed up and through Christ but can help inspire a more profound commitment to what has been revealed through public Revelation. . . .

Jesus Christ, the divine Son of God become man, is the fullness of Revelation by his teaching, witness, death, and Resurrection. On the road to Emmaus, the risen Jesus showed the two disciples how the teachings of the prophets were fulfilled in him and proclaimed by his own lips. Just before his Ascension, Christ commissioned the Apostles to preach the Gospel to all whose hearts would be open to receive them. The revealed Word of God in the Gospel would be for everyone a source of saving truth and moral discipline.

> ### The Paschal Mystery
>
> The word *paschal* refers to Passover. Christ is called the Paschal Lamb because, like the lamb sacrificed during the Passover, whose blood saved the Jews from slaughter, Jesus' sacrifice redeems humanity. The Paschal Mystery concerns Christ's Passion, or suffering, and his death, Resurrection, and Ascension, through which God's plan to save humanity was accomplished. In the Eucharist at Mass, we celebrate and remember the Paschal Mystery.

He commanded the Apostles to proclaim and witness his Kingdom of love, justice, mercy, and healing, foretold by the prophets and fulfilled in his **Paschal Mystery.** Jesus sent them the Holy Spirit to enable them to fulfill this great commission, to give them needed courage, and to help them in their evangelizing work.

Graced by the Holy Spirit, the Apostles did what Jesus commanded them. They did this orally, in writing, by the heroic sanctity of their lives, and by ensuring that there would be successors for this mission. The first communication of the Gospel was by preaching and witness. The Apostles proclaimed Jesus,

> **Paschal Mystery** The work of salvation accomplished by Jesus Christ mainly through his Passion, death, Resurrection, and Ascension.

his Kingdom, and the graces of salvation. They called for the obedience of faith (hearing and obeying God's Word), the reception of Baptism, the formation of a community of believers, gathering for the Eucharist, and generosity to the poor.

The Apostles chose men to be bishops to succeed them and handed on to them "what they received from Jesus' teaching and example and what they learned from the Holy Spirit" (CCC, no. 83). The popes and bishops in union with him are successors of the Apostles and inherit the responsibility of authoritative teaching from them. We call this teaching office the **Magisterium.** "The task of giving an authentic interpretation of the Word of God, whether in its written form or in the form of Tradition, has been entrusted to the living, teaching office of the Church alone" (CCC, no. 85, citing DV, no. 10).

All the faithful share in understanding and handing on revealed truth. "The whole body of the faithful cannot err . . . in matters of belief. This characteristic is shown in the supernatural appreciation of faith *(sensus fidei)* on the part of the whole people, when, 'from the bishops to the last of the faithful,' they manifest a universal consent in matters of faith and morals" (CCC, no. 92, citing Second Vatican Council, *Dogmatic Constitution on the Church* [*Lumen Gentium; LG*], no. 12). Another way of understanding this truth is the principle that the Holy Spirit, dwelling in the Church, draws the whole body of the faithful to believe what truly belongs to the faith. "By this appreciation of the faith, aroused and sustained by the Spirit of truth, the People of God, guided by the sacred teaching authority *(magisterium),* and obeying it, receives not the mere word of men, but truly the word of God (cf. 1 Thes 2:13), the faith once for all delivered to the saints (cf. Jude 3)" (LG, no. 12).

Tradition is the living transmission of the message of the Gospel in the Church. The oral preaching of the Apostles and the written message of salvation under the inspiration of the Holy Spirit (Bible) are conserved and handed on as the Deposit of Faith through the Apostolic Succession in the Church.

Magisterium The Church's living, teaching office, which consists of all the world's bishops, in communion with the Pope.

Both the living Tradition and the written Scriptures have their common source in the revelation of God in Jesus Christ. This is particularly important to understand and believe when one is faced with the postmodern attitude that Tradition cannot be trusted, and that what the Church teaches as Tradition is really just a reflection of particular judgments and biases. Knowing that what Tradition teaches has its ultimate foundation in Jesus Christ helps a person of faith to respond to Tradition with trust. The theological, liturgical, disciplinary, and devotional traditions of the local churches both contain and can be distinguished from this Apostolic Tradition (cf. CCC, Glossary, "Tradition").

Endnotes

1. A covenant was originally a treaty in which an overlord and a vassal accepted certain responsibilities toward each other. In the Old Testament, this idea of covenant became the primary analogy for the relationship between God and his people.

For Reflection

1. The reading states that "God's Revelation unfolded gradually throughout history." What examples in the reading illustrate this point?

2. How does God's Revelation bridge the gulf between us and God?

3. Why is faith essential for recognizing and responding to God's Revelation?

4. Explain how Jesus' commission of the Apostles "to preach the Gospel to all whose hearts would be open to receive them" is continued in the Church today.

2 God Reveals Himself through Creation, Reason, and His Word

Introduction

When Pope John XXIII convened Vatican Council II in 1962, one of his goals was for the Church to reflect on its identity and mission in a rapidly changing world. The era following World War II saw an emerging global economic market, increased exposure to other faith traditions through immigration, an emphasis on science for answers to human problems, and a growing question of the place and practice of faith in the modern world.

Vatican Council II made several changes to the daily practices of Catholics, including allowing the Mass to be said in the local language rather than Latin alone. Documents were produced that addressed different areas of modern life. For example, *Declaration on the Relation of the Church to Non-Christian Religions* (*Nostra Aetate,* 1965) addressed the relationship of the Church to other religions, and *Pastoral Constitution on the Church in the Modern World* (*Gaudium et Spes,* 1965) explored faith and the political sphere. *Dogmatic Constitution on **Divine Revelation*** (*Dei Verbum,* 1965) delved into God's Revelation to humanity through the Scriptures and Tradition and addressed the question "How can we know God?"

Divine Revelation responded to this question by explaining that God reveals himself to humanity through his creation, in the Scriptures, in Tradition, and in the teaching office of the Church, the Magisterium. In a culture that sought to hold science over religion, *Divine*

Divine Revelation God's self-communication and disclosure of the divine plan to humankind through creation, events, persons, and, most fully, Jesus Christ.

18

Revelation countered that the Catholic intellectual tradition and the Scriptures demand that one seek God through both faith and reason. Together, faith and reason are necessary aspects by which we can recognize and encounter God in a substantive relationship of love.

This selection from *Divine Revelation* deals with the question "How can we know about God?" *Divine Revelation* responds to this question, universally asked by humanity throughout time. Additionally, this reading reminds us that the Church, in her earthly ministry, has a duty to manifest the light of Christ and reveal God's plan of salvation to those outside the Catholic faith.

Excerpts from *Dogmatic Constitution on Divine Revelation* (*Dei Verbum*)
By the Second Vatican Council

1. Hearing the word of God with reverence and proclaiming it with faith, the sacred **synod** takes its direction from these words of St. John: "We announce to you the eternal life which dwelt with the Father and was made visible to us. What we have seen and heard we announce to you, so that you may have fellowship with us and our common fellowship be with the Father and His Son Jesus Christ" (1 John 1:2–3). Therefore, following in the footsteps of the Council of Trent and of the First Vatican Council, this present council wishes to set forth authentic **doctrine** on divine revelation and how it is handed on, so that by hearing the message of salvation the whole world may believe, by believing it may hope, and by hoping it may love.

Revelation Itself

2. In His goodness and wisdom God chose to reveal Himself and to make known to us the hidden purpose of

synod A gathering of bishops to discuss important theological issues.

doctrine An official, authoritative teaching of the Church based on the Revelation of God.

His will (see Eph. 1:9) by which through Christ, the Word made flesh, man might in the Holy Spirit have access to the Father and come to share in the divine nature (see Eph. 2:18; 2 Peter 1:4). Through this revelation, therefore, the invisible God (see Col. 1:15, 1 Tim. 1:17) out of the abundance of His love speaks to men as friends (see Ex. 33:11; John 15:14–15) and lives among them (see Bar. 3:38), so that He may invite and take them into fellowship with Himself. This plan of revelation is realized by deeds and words having in inner unity: the deeds wrought by God in the history of salvation manifest and confirm the teaching and realities signified by the words, while the words proclaim the deeds and clarify the mystery contained in them. By this revelation then, the deepest truth about God and the salvation of man shines out for our sake in Christ, who is both the mediator and the fullness of all revelation.

> " In His goodness and wisdom God chose to reveal Himself and to make known to us the hidden purpose of His will . . . "

Prophets

Prophets acted as God's ambassadors to call the Israelites, and even their kings, to follow God's laws and keep his covenant. They conveyed God's messages through poetry, visions, public speeches, and parables. Stories of the prophets Samuel, Nathan, and Elijah can be found in the books of Samuel and Kings. Other prophets' writings can be found in eighteen books in the Old Testament, including Isaiah, Jeremiah, Hosea, and Amos.

3. God, who through the Word creates all things (see John 1:3) and keeps them in existence, gives men an enduring witness to Himself in created realities (see Rom. 1:19–20). Planning to make known the way of heavenly salvation, He went further and from the start manifested Himself to our first parents. Then after their fall His

promise of redemption aroused in them the hope of being saved (see Gen. 3:15) and from that time on He ceaselessly kept the human race in His care, to give eternal life to those who perseveringly do good in search of salvation (see Rom. 2:6–7). Then, at the time He had appointed He called Abraham in order to make of him a great nation (see Gen. 12:2). Through the **patriarchs**, and after them through Moses and the prophets, He taught this people to acknowledge Himself the one living and true God, provident father and just judge, and to wait for the Savior promised by Him, and in this manner prepared the way for the Gospel down through the centuries.

4. Then, after speaking in many and varied ways through the prophets, "now at last in these days God has spoken to us in His Son" (Heb. 1:1–2). For He sent His Son, the eternal Word, who enlightens all men, so that He might dwell among men and tell them of the innermost being of God (see John 1:1–18). Jesus Christ, therefore, the Word made flesh, was sent as "a man to men." He "speaks the words of God" (John 3:34), and completes the work of salvation which His Father gave Him to do (see John 5:36; John 17:4). To see Jesus is to see His Father (John 14:9). For this reason Jesus perfected revelation by fulfilling it through his whole work of making Himself present and manifesting Himself: through His words and deeds, His signs and wonders, but especially through His death and glorious resurrection from the dead and final sending of the Spirit of truth. Moreover He confirmed with divine testimony what revelation proclaimed, that God is with us to free us from the darkness of sin and death, and to raise us up to life eternal.

The Christian dispensation, therefore, as the new and definitive covenant, will never pass away and we now await no further new public revelation before the glorious manifestation of our Lord Jesus Christ (see 1 Tim. 6:14 and Tit. 2:13).

5. "The obedience of faith" (Rom. 13:26; see 1:5;

> **patriarch** The father or leader of a tribe, clan, or tradition. Abraham, Isaac, and Jacob were the patriarchs of the Israelite people.

2 Cor 10:5–6) "is to be given to God who reveals an obedience by which man commits his whole self freely to God, offering the full submission of intellect and will to God who reveals," and freely assenting to the truth revealed by Him. To make this act of faith, the grace of God and the interior help of the Holy Spirit must precede and assist, moving the heart and turning it to God, opening the eyes of the mind and giving "joy and ease to everyone in assenting to the truth and believing it." To bring about an ever deeper understanding of revelation the same Holy Spirit constantly brings faith to completion by His gifts.

6. Through divine revelation, God chose to show forth and communicate Himself and the eternal decisions of His will regarding the salvation of men. That is to say, He chose to share with them those divine treasures which totally transcend the understanding of the human mind.

As a sacred synod has affirmed, God, the beginning and end of all things, can be known with certainty from created reality by the light of human reason (see Rom. 1:20); but teaches that it is through His revelation that those religious truths which are by their nature accessible to human reason can be known by all men with ease, with solid certitude and with no trace of error, even in this present state of the human race.

For Reflection

1. According to the reading, why does God choose "to reveal Himself and to make known to us the hidden purpose of His will"?

2. Explain how God's Revelation is most fully realized in Jesus Christ.

3. What is the role of grace in helping us understand God's Revelation?

3 God's Light Shines in the Human Heart and on the Face of Christ

Introduction

"What is truth?" In the Gospel of John (18:38), Pontius Pilate asks Jesus this question at Jesus' trial, and humanity has pondered the question for ages. The modern and postmodern eras have only underscored the question. Because of the increasing influence and acceptance of **relativism** in modern society, in place of objective truth, it has become harder to point to an objective truth.

Pope John Paul II, a theologian and philosopher, responded to the cultural phenomenon of relativism in 1993 with the **encyclical** *The Splendor of Truth (Veritatis Splendor)*. In this encyclical, he explains that he is writing to address the growing cultural dismissal of truth as an obtainable goal, as well as to address questions regarding some of the Church's foundational moral teachings. He is concerned with the pervasiveness of moral relativism from both outside and within the Church.

This encyclical strategically followed the publication of the *Catechism of the Catholic Church* in 1992, a complete deposit of the Church's teaching, and sought to underscore "the principles of a moral teaching based upon Sacred Scripture and the living Apostolic tradition" (*The Splendor of Truth*, 5).

The arguments found in *The Splendor of Truth* are influenced by John Paul II's life experience

relativism The position that there is no objective truth, only subjective opinions.

encyclical A pastoral letter issued by the Pope to the whole Church and sometimes to the whole world. Encyclicals address important topics, such as the Sacraments, faith, and social issues.

and faith. His belief in objective truth aided him in Nazi-occupied Warsaw, Poland, as he entered an underground seminary to study theology and philosophy. His faith that God's truth is revealed not only in the Scriptures and Tradition but also in creation and in the hearts of all people permeates his theology.

This chapter's reading comes from the introduction to *The Splendor of Truth*. It outlines Pope John Paul II's major reflections on how God's truth is revealed: in the heart and conscience of humanity, in Sacred Scripture and the Tradition of the Church, and in particular, it is reflected in the face of Christ (see 2 Corinthians 3:18).

Excerpt from *The Splendor of Truth* (*Veritatis Splendor*)
By Pope John Paul II

1. Called to salvation through faith in Jesus Christ, "the true light that enlightens everyone" (Jn 1:9), people become "light in the Lord" and "children of light" (Eph 5:8), and are made holy by "obedience to the truth" (1 Pet 1:22).

This obedience is not always easy. As a result of that mysterious original sin, committed at the prompting of Satan, the one who is "a liar and the father of lies" (Jn 8:44), man is constantly tempted to turn his gaze away from the living and true God in order to direct it towards idols (cf. 1 Thes 1:9), exchanging "the truth about God for a lie" (Rom 1:25). Man's capacity to know the truth is also darkened, and his will to submit to it is weakened.

> 66 *Jesus Christ, the "light of the nations," shines upon the face of his Church, which he sends forth to the whole world to proclaim the Gospel to every creature.* 99

Thus, giving himself over to relativism and scepticism (cf. Jn 18:38), he goes off in search of an illusory freedom apart from truth itself.

But no darkness of error or of sin can totally take away from man the light of God the Creator. In the depths of his heart there always remains a yearning for absolute truth and a thirst to attain full knowledge of it. This is eloquently proved by man's tireless search for knowledge in all fields. It is proved even more by his search for the meaning of life. The development of science and technology, this splendid testimony of the human capacity for understanding and for perseverance, does not free humanity from the obligation to ask the ultimate religious questions. Rather, it spurs us on to face the most painful and decisive of struggles, those of the heart and of the moral conscience.

2. No one can escape from the fundamental questions: What must I do? How do I distinguish good from evil? The answer is only possible thanks to the splendour of the truth which shines forth deep within the human spirit, as the Psalmist bears witness: "There are many who say: 'O that we might see some good! Let the light of your face shine on us, O Lord'" (Ps 4:6).

The light of God's face shines in all its beauty on the countenance of Jesus Christ, "the image of the invisible God" (Col 1:15), the "reflection of God's glory" (Heb 1:3), "full of grace and truth" (Jn 1:14). Christ is "the way, and the truth, and the life" (Jn 14:6). Consequently the decisive answer to every one of man's questions, his religious and moral questions in particular, is given by Jesus Christ, or rather is Jesus Christ himself, as the Second Vatican Council recalls: "In fact, it is only in the mystery of the Word incarnate that light is shed on the mystery of man. For Adam, the first man, was a figure of the future man, namely, of Christ the Lord. It is Christ, the last Adam, who fully discloses man to himself and unfolds his noble calling by revealing the mystery of the Father and the Father's love."

Jesus Christ, the "light of the nations," shines upon the face of his Church, which he sends forth to the whole world to proclaim the Gospel to every creature (cf. Mk 16:15). Hence the Church, as the People of God among the nations, while attentive to the new challenges of history and to mankind's efforts to discover the meaning of life, offers to everyone the answer which comes from the truth about Jesus Christ and his Gospel. The Church remains deeply conscious of her "duty in every age of examining the signs of the times and interpreting them in the light of the Gospel, so that she can offer in a manner appropriate to each generation replies to the continual human questionings on the meaning of this life and the life to come and on how they are related."

3. The Church's Pastors, in communion with the Successor of Peter, are close to the faithful in this effort; they guide and accompany them by their authoritative teaching, finding ever new ways of speaking with love and mercy not only to believers but to all people of good will. The Second Vatican Council remains an extraordinary witness of this attitude on the part of the Church which, as an "expert in humanity," places herself at the service of every individual and of the whole world.

The Church knows that the issue of morality is one which deeply touches every person; it involves all people, even those who do not know Christ and his Gospel or God himself. She knows that it is precisely on the path of the moral life that the way of salvation is open to all. The Second Vatican Council clearly recalled this when it stated that "those who without any fault do not know anything about Christ or his Church, yet who search for God with a sincere heart and under the influence of grace, try to put into effect the will of God as known to them through the dictate of conscience . . . can obtain eternal salvation." The Council added: "Nor does divine Providence deny the helps that are necessary for salvation to those who, through no fault of their own, have not yet attained to the express recognition of God, yet who strive, not without divine grace, to lead an upright life. For whatever goodness and truth is found in them is considered by the Church as a preparation for the Gospel and bestowed by him who enlightens everyone that they may in the end have life."

For Reflection

1. The splendor of truth shines deep within the heart of each person and leads to fundamental questions. What questions do you believe draw us closer to God? How can we seek the answers to find truth?

2. Based on this reading, how do we answer the questions: What must I do? How do I distinguish good from evil?

3. Why must the Church examine and interpret the signs of the time in the light of the Gospel?

4 God's Signature in Creation Points to His Existence

Introduction

Saint Thomas Aquinas (ca. 1225–1274), along with Saint Augustine, was one of the most important theologians in Church history. Before joining the Dominican order about 1243, he was educated in the Benedictine order and by Albert the Great, one of the great thinkers of the Middle Ages. Thomas became a doctor of philosophy and theology. At first, his wealthy family opposed his decision to join the Dominicans and even held him captive for months in an attempt to prevent him from joining the order. After a time, they released him. As a Dominican, Thomas taught theology at the renowned University of Paris.

During Thomas's time, the writings of Aristotle had been rediscovered in the West. During his university education, Thomas was exposed to Aristotle's works, as well as those of Arabian writers and thinkers. Thomas was able successfully to explain a number of theological problems by merging meaningful examples from Aristotle and the Arabian thinkers. Thomas's principle of using other sources came from his conviction that any logical conclusion that is true, regardless of who says it, must be from the Holy Spirit. However, this principle provoked tension from a number of his colleagues and his bishop.

In the end, Thomas's work overcame the objections of his critics. His four-volume work, the **Summa Theologicae** (*"Sum of All Theology"*),

> **Summa Theologicae** Literally, "the sum of all theology." One of the most influential works in Catholic theology, written by Thomas Aquinas. Often referred to simply as the Summa.

is considered an authoritative masterpiece of theology that explains many questions surrounding the Apostolic Tradition. One of the most prominent of Thomas's works is his proofs for God's existence. Thomas's proofs presuppose that activity in the world points to something or someone that started that movement. Thomas calls this initial push the "First Cause." The proofs in the world that require and point to such a First Cause include: (1) change in the natural world, (2) creative activity, (3) necessity and interdependence, (4) greatness and perfection, and (5) order in the world that requires a primary director. These are all aspects of the world that individuals can accept as universal truth.

The following reading from Thomas remains important today, because the proofs show that God's existence can be deduced logically through reason and observation of the world. At a time when some people wish to separate faith from reason or religion from science, Thomas teaches us that all serve the same purpose in aiding our reception of God's ongoing Revelation.

Excerpts from *Summa Theologicae*

By Saint Thomas Aquinas

Whether God's Existence Can Be Demonstrated

There are two types of demonstration. There is demonstration through the cause, or, as we say, "from grounds," which argues from cause to effect. There is also demonstration by means of effects, following the order in which we experience things, arguing from effect to cause. Now when an effect is more apparent to us than its cause, we come to know the cause through its effect. Even though the effect should be better known to us, we can demonstrate from any effect that its cause exists, because effects always depend on some cause, and a cause must exist if its effect exists. We can therefore demonstrate that God exists from what is not evident to us on the basis of effects which are evident to us. . . .

Whether God Exists

The existence of God can be proved in five ways. The first and most obvious **proof** is the argument from change *[ex parte motus]*. It is clearly the case that some things in this world are in the process of changing. Now everything that is in the process of being changed is changed by something else, since nothing is changed unless it is potentially that towards which it is being changed, whereas that which changes is actual. To change something is nothing else than to bring it from potentiality to actuality, and a thing can be brought from potentiality to actuality only by something which is actual. Thus a fire, which is actually hot, makes wood, which is potentially hot, to be actually hot, thus changing and altering it. Now it is impossible for the same thing to be both actual and potential in the same respect, although it may be so in different respects. What is actually hot cannot at the same time be potentially hot, although it is potentially cold. It is therefore impossible that, in the same manner and in the same way, anything should be both the one which effects a change and the one that is changed, so that it should change itself. Whatever is changed must therefore be changed by something else. If, then, whatever is changing it is itself changed, this also must be changed by

> ### Aristotle
>
> The ancient Greek philosopher Plato (ca. 427–347 BC) and his student Aristotle (384–322 BC) were two of the most influential philosophers of ancient Greece. They wrote on a wide range of topics, including the creation and form of the world, order in nature, ethics, and rhetoric. Aristotle's writings in particular established a comprehensive system of Western philosophy, encompassing morality and aesthetics, logic and science, and politics and metaphysics that still influences Western society today.

> **proof** A step-by-step explanation of a thesis with support and a logical conclusion that points to objective knowledge. Often found in philosophy.

something else, and this in turn by something else again. But this cannot go on forever, since there would then be no first cause to this process of change, and consequently no other agent of change, because secondary things which change cannot change unless they are changed by a first cause, in the same way as a stick cannot move unless it is moved by the hand. We are therefore bound to arrive at a first cause of change which is not changed by anything, and everyone understands that this is God.

The second way is based on the nature of an efficient cause. We find that there is a sequence of efficient causes in the observable world. But we do not find that anything is the efficient cause of itself. Nor is this possible, for the thing would then be prior to itself, which is impossible. But neither can the sequence of efficient causes be infinite, for in every sequence the first efficient cause is the cause of an intermediate cause, and an intermediate cause is the cause of the ultimate cause, whether there are many intermediate causes, or just one. Now when a cause is taken away, so is its effect. Hence if there were no first efficient cause, there would be no ultimate cause, and no intermediate cause. But if there was an infinite regression of efficient causes, there would be no first efficient cause. As a result, there would be no ultimate effect, and no intermediate causes. But this is plainly false. We are therefore bound to suppose that there is a first efficient cause. And everyone calls this "God."

The third way is from the nature of possibility and necessity. There are some things which may either exist or not exist, since some things come to be and pass away, and may therefore exist or not exist. Now it is impossible that all of these should exist at all times, because there is at least some time when that which may possibly not exist does not exist. Hence if all things were such that they might not exist, at some time or other there would be nothing. But if this were true there would be nothing in existence now, since what does not exist cannot begin to exist, unless through something which does exist. If nothing had ever existed, it would have been impossible for anything to begin to exist, and there would now be nothing at all. But this is plainly false, and hence not all existence is merely possible. Something in things must be necessary. Now everything which is necessary either derives its necessity from somewhere else or does not. But we cannot go on to infinity with necessary things which have a cause of their necessity, any more than with efficient causes, as we proved. We are therefore bound to suppose something necessary in itself, which does not owe its necessity to anything else, but which is the cause of the necessity of other things. And everyone calls this "God."

The fourth way is from the gradation that occurs in things, which are found to be more good, true, noble and so on, just as others are found to be less so. Things are said to be more and less because they approximate in different degrees to that which is greatest. A thing gets hotter and hotter as it approaches the thing which is the hottest. There is therefore something which is the truest, the best, and the noblest, and which is consequently the greatest in being, since that which has the greatest truth is also greatest in being. . . . Now that which most thoroughly possesses the nature of any genus is the cause of all that the genus contains. Thus fire, which is most perfectly hot, is the cause of all hot things. . . . There is therefore something which is the cause of the being of all things that are, as well as of their goodness and their every perfection. This we call "God."

> ❝ *There is therefore something which is the cause of the being of all things that are, as well as of their goodness and their every perfection. This we call "God."* ❞

The fifth way is based on the governance of things. We see how some things, like natural bodies, work for an end even though they have no knowledge. The fact that they nearly always operate in the same way, and so as to achieve the maximum good, makes this obvious, and shows that they attain their end by design, not by chance. Now things which have no knowledge tend towards an end only through the agency of something which knows and also understands, as in the case of an arrow which requires an archer. There is therefore an intelligent being by whom all natural things are directed to their end. This we call "God."

For Reflection

1. Based on this reading, explain how knowing or witnessing an effect helps us know the cause of that effect.

2. Identify and summarize the five proofs Thomas identified for the existence of God.

3. What examples have you observed from the order and beauty in nature and creation that point toward the existence of God?

5 The Personal Character of Christian Faith

Introduction

Joseph Ratzinger grew up in Germany while Hitler was in power. He excelled in philosophy and theology in school and, following ordination as a priest, was one of the youngest theologian observers at Vatican Council II. His peers considered him an outstanding scholar, and he taught at some of the most prestigious theological schools in Germany. He was named Archbishop of Munich and Freising by John Paul II and later became cardinal and was appointed to head the **Congregation for the Doctrine of the Faith** (CDF). While in this position, he wrote many important introductions to theological statements from the Vatican and the Pontifical Biblical Commission.

Following the death of Pope John Paul II in April 2005, Cardinal Ratzinger was elected Pope and took the name Benedict XVI. He entered the papacy as the Church faced many difficulties: a sexual abuse scandal, a dwindling Catholic population in Europe, and the view in some circles that the Church required a renewal of its identity. Aware of these and other challenges facing the Church, Ratzinger selected the name Benedict in reference to Benedict of Nursia and Pope Benedict XV. Benedict of Nursia undertook great works of evangelization that contributed to the spread of Christianity in the West, and Pope Benedict XV worked to promote peace and build Christian unity. Evangelization and working for Christian unity are two ways Pope Benedict XVI hoped to address the challenges facing the Church.

Congregation for the Doctrine of the Faith An agency in the Vatican that oversees matters of doctrine for the entire Catholic Church.

Pope Benedict XVI's first encyclical, *God Is Love*, engaged these problems by emphasizing God's selfless love that is poured out to humanity in the covenant and Christ. He concluded the encyclical with a long meditation on what God's love demands in return from those who receive it. In his third encyclical, *Charity in Truth*, Pope Benedict reengaged the issues of poverty, ethics, and social justice in the midst of growing materialism and the outbreak of global economic hardship.

These topics showed Pope Benedict XVI to be a leader who embraced opportunities to teach and deepen the understanding of the faithful of God's extraordinary gift of love and the requirements of discipleship that are modeled in Christ's selfless giving of himself for us.

Before he became Pope, Cardinal Ratzinger was a renowned theologian with many publications. One of his most popular books was a reflection on the Nicene Creed—the foundational expression of Christian faith—titled *Introduction to Christianity*. The reading that follows is a selection from this book.

In this reading Ratzinger emphasizes the fundamental personal character of Christian faith—namely, that Christianity does not profess belief in some*thing*, but rather in some*one*. This someone in whom we believe finds its fullest expression in the person of Jesus Christ, who personally demonstrates that the ultimate meaning of the world is found in selfless giving to others. Faith in the person of Jesus offers believers the comfort that God objectively loves and knows them and wishes to offer them eternal glory with him.

This reading is important today because our culture tends to commercialize and focus on material gain in all things—even faith. In the era of megachurches and wanting to "win" in religion as in politics and other arenas in society, this reading reminds us that faith in Christ is not a thing that must be attained, but rather it is the giving of oneself to believe in the person of Jesus Christ, in whom we see God most clearly.

Excerpt from *Introduction to Christianity*

By Cardinal Joseph Ratzinger / Pope Benedict XVI

7. "I Believe in You"

In all that has been said so far the most fundamental feature of Christian faith or belief has still not been specified; namely, its personal character. Christian faith is more than the option in favor of a spiritual ground to the world; its central formula is not "I believe in something," but "I believe in you."[1] It is the encounter with the man Jesus, and in this encounter it experiences the meaning of the world as a person. In Jesus' life from the Father, in the immediacy and intensity of his converse with him in prayer and, indeed, face to face, he is God's witness, through whom the intangible has become tangible, the distant has drawn near. And further: he is not simply the witness whose evidence we trust when he tells us what he has seen in an existence that had really made the complete about-turn from a false contentment with the foreground of life to the depths of the whole truth; he is the presence of the eternal itself in this world. In his life, in the unconditional devotion of himself to

> **He is the presence of the eternal itself in this world.**

men, the meaning of the world is present before us; it vouchsafes itself to us as love that loves even me and makes life worth living by this incomprehensible gift of a love free from any threat of fading away or any tinge of egoism. The meaning of the world is the "you," though only the one that is not itself an open question but rather the ground of all, which needs no other ground.

Thus faith is the finding of a "you" that upholds me and amid all the unfulfilled—and in the last resort unfulfillable—hope of human encounters gives me the promise of an indestructible love that not only longs for eternity but also guarantees it. Christian faith lives on the discovery that not only is there such a thing as objective meaning but that this meaning knows me and loves me, that I can entrust myself to it like the child who knows that everything he may be wondering about is safe in the "you" of

> **John the Baptist**
>
> John the Baptist was a cousin of Jesus and a prophet who preached repentance and baptized those who sought forgiveness for their sins. He acts as the herald for Jesus by announcing the arrival of God's Kingdom and preparing the Lord's path (see Matthew 3:1, Isaiah 40:3, Mark 1:2–3, 3:1–10). Ancient Jewish and pagan historians even mention the numbers of people who traveled to the Jordan to hear John preach.

his mother. Thus in the last analysis believing, trusting, and loving are one, and all the theses around which belief revolves are only concrete expressions of the all-embracing about-turn, of the assertion "I believe in you"—of the discovery of God in the countenance of the man Jesus of Nazareth.

Of course, this does not do away with the need for reflection, as we have already seen earlier. "Are you really he?" This question was asked anxiously in a dark hour even by John the Baptist, the prophet who had directed his own disciples to the rabbi from Nazareth and recognized him as the greater, for whom he could only prepare the way. Are you really he? The believer will repeatedly experience the darkness in which the contradiction of unbelief surrounds him like a gloomy prison from which there is no escape, and the indifference of the world, which goes its way unchanged as if nothing had happened, seems only to mock his hope. We have to pose the question, "Are you really he?" not only out of intellectual honesty and because of reason's responsibility, but also in accordance with the interior law of love, which wants to know more and more him to whom it has given its Yes, so as to be able to love him more. Are you really he? Ultimately, all the reflections contained in this book are subordinate to this question and thus revolve around the basic form of the confession: "I believe in you, Jesus of Nazareth, as the meaning **(logos)** of the world and of my life."

> *logos* A Greek word meaning "word." *Logos* is a title of Jesus Christ found in the Gospel of John that illuminates the relationship between the Three Persons of the Holy Trinity (see John 1:1,14).

Endnotes

1. Cf. H. Fries, Glauben-Wissen (Berlin, 1960), especially pp. 84–95; J. Mouroux, Ich glaube an dich (Einsiedeln, 1951); C. Cirne-Lima, Der personale Glaube (Innsbruck, 1959).

For Reflection

1. The phrase *I believe in you* encourages an intimate relationship with God and the person of Christ. Based on this reading, how does the saying *I believe in you* encourage an intimate relationship with God in the person of Christ?

2. Cardinal Ratzinger states, "believing, trusting, and loving are one." What does he mean by this statement?

3. How does belief in and a personal relationship with Christ help us deal with doubts and difficult times?

Part 2
About Sacred Scripture

6 Searching for God Requires Both Faith and Reason

Introduction

Karol Wojtyla was born in 1920 in the Polish town of Wadowice. In 1938 he and his father moved to Krakow, where he began his studies at the Jagiellonian University. The next year Nazi forces closed the university. During the Nazi occupation of Poland he attended an underground seminary and was ordained to the priesthood in 1946 before receiving doctorates in philosophy (1948) and theology (1953). At the age of 38, he was appointed auxiliary bishop of Krakow. He later participated in the Second Vatican Council (see chapter 2). When he was elected Pope in 1978, at the age of 58, he became the first non-Italian to hold that position in more than four centuries. He went on to become the second-longest-reigning Pope in documented history.

During his twenty-five-year pontificate, Pope John Paul II composed fourteen papal encyclicals, wrote numerous other apostolic letters, and became the most-traveled Pope in history by visiting more one hundred countries. He also became extremely influential in world politics.

Pope John Paul II wrote the encyclical *On the Relationship Between Faith and Reason (Fides et Ratio)* to respond to what he called "a crisis of meaning" in Western civilization. This is in many ways the same situation of relativism to which *The Splendor of Truth* responded. But whereas *The Splendor of Truth* sought to show where truth can be found, *Faith and Reason* sought to explain the means by which truth is found.

The reading in this chapter, from *Faith and Reason,* addresses the study of the Scriptures and theology in light of their goals of finding and proclaiming the ultimate truth. In the Scriptures God reveals himself as absolute and humanity as created in his glorious image. God also teaches his commands of how to live. The Church is responsible for proclaiming this good news through two ways: faith (theology) and reason (philosophy). To convey the truth effectively to the world, the Gospel should be taught so it is both believed and understood.

In *Faith and Reason,* Pope John Paul II encourages Christians to be committed to a vibrant method of conveying truth to others. In this way the Church may communicate God's saving plan to every new generation. The vibrancy that contributes to this successful evangelization involves a focus on the Trinity and God's outpouring of himself in the Incarnation. Christians today must also be able to convey the truth through faith and reason to teach the Good News effectively.

Excerpt from *On the Relationship Between Faith and Reason (Fides et Ratio)*

By Pope John Paul II

The indispensable requirements of the word of God

80. In Sacred Scripture are found elements, both implicit and explicit, which allow a vision of the human being and the world which has exceptional philosophical density. Christians have come to an ever deeper awareness of the wealth to be found in the sacred text. It is there that we learn that what we experience is not absolute: it is neither uncreated nor self-generating. God alone is the Absolute. From the Bible there emerges also a vision of man as ***imago Dei.*** This vision offers indications regarding man's life, his freedom and the immortality of the human spirit. Since the created world is not self-sufficient, every illusion of autonomy which would deny the essential dependence on God of every creature—the human being included—leads to dramatic situations which subvert the rational search for the harmony and the meaning of human life.

> ***imago Dei*** Latin for "image of God."

The problem of moral evil—the most tragic of evil's forms—is also addressed in the Bible, which tells us that such evil stems not from any material deficiency, but is a wound inflicted by the disordered exercise of human freedom. In the end, the word of God poses the problem of the meaning of life and proffers its response in directing the human being to Jesus Christ, the Incarnate Word of God, who is the perfect realization of human existence. A reading of the sacred text would reveal other aspects of this problem; but what emerges clearly is the rejection of all forms of relativism, materialism and pantheism.

The fundamental conviction of the "philosophy" found in the Bible is that the world and human life do have a meaning and look towards their fulfilment, which comes in Jesus Christ. The mystery of the Incarnation will always remain the central point of reference for an understanding of the enigma of human existence, the created world and God himself. The challenge of this mystery pushes philosophy to its limits, as reason is summoned to make its own a logic which brings down the walls within which it risks being confined. Yet only at this point does the meaning of life reach its defining moment. The intimate essence of God and of the human being become intelligible: in the mystery of the Incarnate Word, human nature and divine nature are safeguarded in all their autonomy, and at the same time the unique bond which sets them together in mutuality without confusion of any kind is revealed. . . .

92. As an understanding of Revelation, theology has always had to respond in different historical moments to the demands of different cultures, in order then to mediate the content of faith to those cultures in a coherent and conceptually clear way. Today, too, theology faces a dual task. On the one hand, it must be increasingly committed to the task entrusted to it by the Second Vatican Council, the task of renewing its specific methods in order to serve evangelization more effectively. How can we fail to recall in this regard the words of Pope John XXIII at the opening of the Council? He said then: "In line with the keen expectation of those who sincerely love the Christian, Catholic and apostolic religion, this doctrine must be known more widely and deeply, and souls must be instructed and formed in it more completely; and this certain and un-changeable doctrine, always to be faithfully respected, must be understood

more profoundly and presented in a way which meets the needs of our time."

On the other hand, theology must look to the ultimate truth which Revelation entrusts to it, never content to stop short of that goal. Theologians should remember that their work corresponds "to a dynamism found in the faith itself" and that the proper object of their enquiry is "the Truth which is the living God and his plan for salvation revealed in Jesus Christ." This task, which is theology's prime concern, challenges philosophy as well. The array of problems which today need to be tackled demands a joint effort—approached, it is true, with different methods—so that the truth may once again be known and expressed. The Truth, which is Christ, imposes itself as an all-embracing authority which holds out to theology and philosophy alike the prospect of support, stimulation and increase (cf. Eph 4:15).

To believe it possible to know a universally valid truth is in no way to encourage intolerance; on the contrary, it is the essential condition for sincere and authentic dialogue between persons. On this basis alone is it possible to overcome divisions and to journey together towards full truth, walking those paths known only to the Spirit of the Risen Lord. I wish at this point to indicate the specific form which the call to unity now takes, given the current tasks of theology.

93. The chief purpose of theology is to provide an understanding of Revelation and the content of faith. The very heart of theological enquiry will thus be the contemplation of the mystery of the Triune God. The approach to this mystery begins with reflection upon the mystery of the Incarnation of the Son of God: his coming as man, his going to his Passion and Death, a mystery issuing into his glorious Resurrection and Ascension to the right hand of the Father, whence he would send the Spirit of truth to bring his Church to birth and give her growth. From this vantage-point, the prime commitment of theology is seen to be the understanding of God's *kenosis,* a grand and mysterious truth for the human mind, which finds it inconceivable that suffering and death can express a love

> *kenosis* Greek for "outpouring." Often used to describe God's outpouring of his love or to Christ's sacrifice on the cross.

which gives itself and seeks nothing in return. In this light, a careful analysis of texts emerges as a basic and urgent need: first the texts of Scripture, and then those which express the Church's living Tradition. On this score, some problems have emerged in recent times, problems which are only partially new; and a coherent solution to them will not be found without philosophy's contribution.

94. An initial problem is that of the relationship between meaning and truth. Like every other text, the sources which the theologian interprets primarily transmit a meaning which needs to be grasped and explained. This meaning presents itself as the truth about God which God himself communicates through the sacred text. Human language thus embodies the language of God, who communicates his own truth with that wonderful "condescension" which mirrors the logic of the Incarnation. In interpreting the sources of Revelation, then, the theologian needs to ask what is the deep and authentic truth which the texts wish to communicate, even within the limits of language.

The truth of the biblical texts, and of the Gospels in particular, is certainly not restricted to the narration of simple historical events or the statement of neutral facts, as historicist positivism would claim. Beyond simple historical occurrence, the truth of the events which these texts relate lies rather in the meaning they have in and for the history of salvation. This truth is elaborated fully in the Church's constant reading of these texts over the centuries, a reading which preserves intact their original meaning. There is a pressing need, therefore, that the relationship between fact and meaning, a relationship which constitutes the specific sense of history, be examined also from the philosophical point of view.

95. The word of God is not addressed to any one people or to any one period of history. Similarly, dogmatic statements, while reflecting at times the culture of the period in which they were defined, formulate an unchanging and ultimate truth. This prompts the question of how one can reconcile the absoluteness and the universality of truth with the unavoidable historical and cultural conditioning of the formulas which express that truth. The claims of historicism, I noted earlier, are untenable; but the use of a hermeneutic open to the appeal of metaphysics can show how it is possible to move from the historical and contingent circumstances in which the texts developed to the truth which they express, a truth transcending those circumstances.

> " *Truth can never be confined to time and culture; in history it is known, but it also reaches beyond history.* "

Human language may be conditioned by history and constricted in other ways, but the human being can still express truths which surpass the phenomenon of language. Truth can never be confined to time and culture; in history it is known, but it also reaches beyond history.

For Reflection

1. John Paul II wrote the encyclical *Faith and Reason* as a response to a "crisis of meaning" and to relativism in place of objective truth. How can faith and reason help us pursue objective truth?

2. What does it mean to say that the Word of God is not intended for one specific group of people?

3. In light of this reading, explain Pope John Paul II's statement, "Truth can never be confined to time and culture; in history it is known, but it also reaches beyond history."

7 God Reveals Himself in History and Scripture

Introduction

Avery Dulles, SJ, was one of the foremost contemporary theologians in America. He published dozens of books on Revelation, the Church and society, and other theological topics. Pope John Paul II appointed Dulles a cardinal of the Catholic Church on February 21, 2001, making him the first American-born theologian who is not a bishop to receive this honor.

The reading for this chapter comes from Dulles's book *Revelation Theology*. In it he outlines ways God reveals himself to humanity. The selection concerns how God is revealed in the course of human history and through the Scriptures. Through the Scriptures God reveals his saving actions throughout history and shows that he cares for and is intimately involved with his creation.

God intervenes in history when necessary. In the Old Testament he does this by summoning Abraham and then later by making a covenant with the Israelites after freeing them from slavery in Egypt.

In the New Testament, God reveals himself in an entirely new way, as Christ. Through Christ he has initiated a new Exodus from sin and death and a renewal of creation as a whole. Now God speaks not merely through intermediaries but also through his Son, whose sacrifice saves and whose teachings allow the faithful to live as a people sanctified to God.

The following selection from Dulles is important because it traces the Revelation of God in the unified witness of the Scriptures, as well as in history. In this reading Dulles demonstrates that God's Word is one that speaks to people not in past texts alone but also in the daily life of human history.

Excerpt from *Revelation Theology*

By Avery Dulles

Summarizing the Old Testament view of revelation, one may say that **Yahweh** progressively manifests himself, through word and work, as Lord of history. He freely raises up spokesmen of his own choosing, whether patriarchs such as Abraham, national heroes such as Moses, or prophets and seers such as Samuel, Isaiah, and Ezekiel. He entrusts them with messages which they are to deliver to others, often to the whole people. Although the universal significance of Israelite religion is sometimes suggested (especially in **Deutero-Isaiah**), the horizons are for the most part particular, insofar as the revelation is addressed to a single nation. The Israelite faith is also inchoative, insofar as it is in tension toward a greater and definitive manifestation yet to come. While often accompanied by miraculous **theophanies**, dreams, and visions, revelation for the Old Testament writers is primarily to be found in the "word of God." The word, however, is not mere speculative speech. It refers to the concrete history of Israel, which it recalls and interprets. It commemorates God's previous dealings with his people and includes promises for the future, thus arousing faith and hope. The word of God, moreover, is powerful and dynamic; it produces a transforming encounter with the Lord who utters it, and imposes stringent demands on the recipient. It opens up to him a new way of life, pregnant with new possibilities of punishment and deliverance. Revelation is ultimately aimed to bring blessings upon the whole nation, including peace, prosperity, and holiness.

Yahweh The most sacred of the Old Testament names for God, which he revealed to Moses. It is frequently translated as "I AM" or "I am who am."

Deutero-Isaiah A name used to describe the author of chapters 40–55 of the Book of Isaiah, who wrote around 500 BC.

theophany God's manifestation of himself in a visible form to enrich human understanding of him. An example is God's appearance to Moses in the form of a burning bush (see Exodus 3:4–17).

Theophany

Theophany is the term used to describe God's manifestation of himself in a visible way so individuals and communities might better understand him. Theophanies are profound experiences through which God dramatically alters human life. God's appearance to Moses in the burning bush is possibly the most-referenced Old Testament example of a theophany, but there are numerous others. From God's appearances to Abraham (see Genesis 12:7 and 12:14–17), Jacob (see Genesis 28:13–15), and Moses and the Israelites (see Exodus 19:18-19), to his communications with the prophets (see Isaiah 6:1–8, Jeremiah 1:4–19, and Ezekiel 1:27–28), God continually has broken into the human world so we might better know him. Theophanies are not confined to the Old Testament. In the New Testament, we find examples of theophanies in the appearance of the angel Gabriel to Mary (see Luke 1:26–38), the appearance of the Spirit of God at the baptism of Jesus (see Matthew 3:16–17), and the appearance of Jesus to Saul on the road to Damascus (see Acts 9:1–9).

B. The New Testament

As in other matters, so in the notion of revelation, the New Testament takes up the themes enunciated in the Old Testament, draws them together, and brings them to a higher and unforseen fulfilment. "All these writings of ancient Israel, both those which are concerned with her past relationship to God and those which dealt with her future one, were seen by Jesus Christ, and certainly by the Apostles and the early Church, as a collection of predictions which pointed to him, the saviour of Israel and of the world."[1] The heart of the New Testament is that the definitive, universal revelation is given to mankind in Jesus, to be authoritatively proclaimed by the Church to all nations until the end of time (Mt. 28:18–20). The Old Testament affirmation that God spoke to man "face to face, as a man speaks to his friend" (Ex. 33:11) was surpassingly fulfilled in the coming of God's own Son (Jn. 1:17–18). The best summary of the New Testament view of revelation, as related to the Old Testament, is Hebrews 1:1–2: "In many and various ways God spoke of old to our fathers by the prophets; but in these last days he has spoken to us by a Son,

> " *The heart of the New Testament is that the definitive, universal revelation is given to mankind in Jesus.* "

whom he appointed the heir of all things, through whom also he created the world." . . .

Jesus as Son is thus the revealer of the Father and his plans. The central theme of the revelation is the arrival of the **Kingdom**, which is understood as involving all the blessings foretold by the Law, the Prophets, and the Psalms. The apostles are the chosen recipients of this revelation, notwithstanding their lack of personal qualifications (Mt. 11:25). They are freely called by Jesus, enlightened by the grace of the Father (Mt. 16:17), instructed by Jesus regarding the true nature of the Kingdom, and appointed to go and preach in his name. . . .

Drawing together the various strands of the New Testament conception of revelation, we may offer the following general description:

(a) It is a completely gratuitous disclosure of God's mind and purposes, salvific in intent. God freely decides to publish the good news of his redemptive will toward all mankind, and raises up "vessels of election" (see Acts 9:15) to herald the message.

(b) The apostles take the place of the prophets as God's chief heralds (Mt. 28:19; Lk. 24:48; Acts 1:8; Jn. 17:20; and so forth).

(c) The revelation is to be proclaimed to all mankind, as is evident from the same texts. To the universality of the gospel there corresponds a universal need on the part of mankind. Although in times past God may have been satisfied with a vague and undetermined kind of worship, which attained God only as one unknown (Acts 17:23.30–31), now the time has come for men to repent and to call upon Jesus as universal Saviour (Rom. 10:12–18; Rom. 16:26; 1 Tim. 2:3–7).

(d) The revelation is final, in the sense that it fulfills the whole economy of the Old Testament and ushers in the last age of the world (Heb. 1:1–2; Eph. 1:10). Believing Christians have already received this

> **Kingdom** The culmination or goal of God's plan of salvation, the Kingdom (or Kingdom of God) is announced by the Gospel and present in Jesus Christ. The Kingdom is the reign or rule of God over the hearts of people and, as a consequence of that, the development of a new social order based on unconditional love. The fullness of God's Kingdom will not be realized until the end of time. Also called the Reign of God or the Kingdom of Heaven.

revelation (Rom. 16:25f.; 1 Cor. 2:10; Eph. 3:3.5). Yet revelation continues to occur, insofar as we are still living in the last times (1 Cor. 14:30; Phil. 4:15; Jn. 16:13). So obscure is our apprehension of the divine truth in this life, that it falls far short of the face-to-face vision for which we hope (1 Cor. 13:12). In many New Testament texts, therefore, the term "reveal" is used in the future tense, with reference to the consummation of history, including the revelation of the man of sin (2 Thess. 2:3.8) and the return of the Son of Man (Lk. 17:30). In the "Day of the Lord," as understood by Paul, there will be a revelation of God's wrath against sinners (Rom. 2:5), the salvation of the faithful (Rom. 8:19), and the glory of Christ with his saints (Col. 3:4; 2 Thess. 1:10). In Johannine language, the life which is announced by the witnesses of Christ will not be seen as it truly is until he appears at the end (1 Jn. 3:2).

(e) The revelation is communicated through a combination of words and deeds. Paul and Hebrews accentuate the idea that revelation is a word demanding the obedience of faith. Yet, in the gospels, Christ reveals not only by his preaching and teaching (Mk. 1:14f.; Jn. 6:63.14:10), but also by his symbolic actions, such as cleansing the Temple, embracing little children, cursing the barren fig tree, and the like. Many of his miracles, such as the multiplication of the loaves and fishes, and the healing of the deaf mute, may be regarded as **parables** in action. From the point of view of faith, all that Christ did is instructive and revelatory. As Augustine put it in a famous text, "Because Christ himself is the Word of God, the very deed of the Word is a word to us."[2]

parables Simple stories that use everyday images to communicate a religious or moral lesson.

Endnotes

1. G. von Rad, *Old Testament Theology,* 2 (New York: 1965) 319.
2. *Tract. in Ioh.* 24:1 (CC 36:244).

For Reflection

1. Which major figures from the Old Testament are mentioned in the selection, and how do they demonstrate God's lessons to Israel and his saving plan for humanity?

2. Explain what you think Dulles meant when he wrote "the New Testament takes up the themes enunciated in the Old Testament, draws them together, and brings them to a higher and unforseen fulfilment."

3. Summarize part e of the reading, which begins, "The revelation is communicated through a combination of words and deeds."

8 Scripture Study Reveals God's Word

Introduction

The early Church (about AD 200–500) was divided geographically and culturally between the Latin West and the Greek East. For more than two hundred years, the Greek scholars of the Eastern half dominated the development and teaching of theology and the Scriptures. One reason was that the Scriptures and most theological texts were written primarily in Greek—a single, complete Bible in Latin did not yet exist.

Enter Saint Jerome (ca. AD 340–420). Jerome was a well-educated priest and scholar who was commissioned by Pope Damasus I to translate the Bible from the original Hebrew and Greek into Latin, revising earlier fragments of Latin translations by others. This translation, which became known as the Vulgate, was the first major Latin translation of the Bible. The Vulgate became the official text used by Latin Scripture scholars, and it eventually became the translation the Church used for the readings in the liturgy. Along with the **Vulgate**, Jerome wrote commentaries in Latin examining many books in the Bible. His emphasis on placing study of the Scriptures at the center of one's spiritual life renewed interest in biblical studies for centuries to come in the West. Jerome expressed the importance of studying the Scriptures when he stated, "Ignorance of Scripture is ignorance of Christ." Today the Church honors Jerome as the patron saint of Scripture scholars.

Vulgate The first complete Latin translation of the Bible, which became standard in the Roman Catholic Church for use in the liturgy and in publications of the Scriptures.

This reading from a letter written by Saint Jerome in AD 394 to Paulinus, the bishop of Nola, concerns the importance of the Scriptures in the spirituality of the individual believer. In particular, it deals with how one may find Christ throughout all of the Scriptures through careful study. Although Christ existed before time, he was not completely revealed in the course of human history until the Incarnation, although, as this reading notes, he "remains hidden in a mystery." Yet because of the Spirit, the authors of the Old Testament can be seen pointing forward to Christ's arrival to save humanity. Early Christian preachers and the Apostles cited the Old Testament as evidence that Jesus was the Christ and the Son of God and that his death brought salvation for those who believe (for example, see Acts 2:17–34, 3:22–24, 1 Cor 10:1–4, 2 Cor 3:1–6, 1 Pet 2:1–10).

This reading is relevant today because it describes how all of Scripture reveals God's Word about salvation. Jerome's words remind us that our understanding of Christ and our salvation in him are greatly promoted through the study of the Scriptures.

Excerpt from *Letter 53*

By Saint Jerome

[Paul] speaks of a "wisdom of God hidden in a mystery, which God ordained before the world" (1 Corinthians 2: 7). God's wisdom is Christ, for Christ, we are told, is "the power of God and the wisdom of God" (1 Corinthians 1: 30). This wisdom remains hidden in a mystery. It is to this that the title of Psalm 9: 1, "for the hidden things of the Son," refers. In him are hidden all the treasures of wisdom and knowledge. The one who was hidden in mystery is the same who was predestined before the world, and was foreordained and prefigured in the **Law** and the Prophets. That is why the prophets

> **Law** The first five books of the Bible (Genesis, Exodus, Leviticus, Numbers, and Deuteronomy), also called the Torah, which contain God's covenant with Israel.

The Suffering Servant

In the story of the eunuch from the Acts of the Apostles (8:26–40), the eunuch ponders the words of the prophet in Isaiah, chapter 35:

Like a sheep he was led to the slaughter,

and as a lamb before its shearer is silent,

so he opened not his mouth.

In [his] humiliation justice was denied him.

Who will tell of his posterity?

For his life is taken from the earth.

(Acts 8:32–33)

In the passage Isaiah prophesies about the suffering servant who is without sin and who, through the acceptance of his suffering and death, makes amends for the sins of his people. Philip, in explaining this passage to the eunuch, helps the eunuch see that Isaiah's prophecy of the suffering servant finds its complete fulfillment in Jesus Christ.

were called seers: they saw him whom others did not see. Abraham also saw his day, and was glad (John 8: 56). The heavens which were sealed to a rebellious people were opened to Ezekiel (Ezekiel 1: 1). "Open my eyes," says David, "so that I may behold the wondrous things of your law" (Psalm 118: 18). For the law is spiritual, and in order to understand it we need the veil to be removed and the glory of God to be seen with an uncovered face (2 Corinthians 3: 14–18). . . .

In the Acts of the Apostles, the holy **eunuch** . . . was reading Isaiah, when he was asked by Philip: "Do you understand what you are reading?" "How can I," he replied, "unless someone teaches me?" (Acts 8: 30–31). I am no more holy nor more learned than this eunuch, who was from Ethiopia, that is from the ends of the world. He left a royal court and went as far as the temple; and such was his love for divine knowledge that he was reading the Holy Scriptures while in his chariot. Yet even though he was holding a book in his hand and was reflecting on the words of the Lord, even sounding them with his tongue

eunuch A castrated male slave serving in a royal court.

and pronouncing them with his lips [*lingua volveret, labiis personaret*], he did not know who he was worshiping in this book. Then Philip came, and showed him Jesus hidden in the letter [*qui clausus latebat in littera*]. What a marvelous teacher! In the same hour the eunuch believed and was baptized. He became one of the faithful and a saint. From being a pupil he became a master. He found more in the desert spring of the church than he had done in the gilded temple of the synagogue. . . .

This matter I have dealt with only briefly—I could not manage any more within the limits of a letter—so that you will understand that you cannot advance in the Holy Scriptures unless you have an experienced guide to show you the way. . . .

I beg you, my dearest brother, to live among these [sacred books], to meditate on them, to know nothing else, to seek nothing else. Does not this seem to you to be a little bit of heaven here on earth [*in terris regni caelestis habitaculum*]? Do not take offence on account of the simplicity of Holy Scripture or the un-sophistication of its words [*quasi vilitate verborum*], for these are due either to translation faults or have some deeper purpose. For

> ❝ *So let us study here on earth that knowledge which will continue with us in heaven.* ❞

Scripture offers itself in such a way that an uneducated congregation can more easily learn from it, some benefit there, and both the learned and the unlearned can discover different meanings in the same sentence. I am not so arrogant nor so forward as to claim that I know this, which would be like wanting to pick on earth the fruits of trees whose roots are in heaven. However, I confess that I would like to do so. . . . The Lord has said: "ask, and it shall be given: knock, and it shall be opened; seek, and you will find" (Matthew 7: 7). So let us study here on earth that knowledge which will continue with us in heaven.

For Reflection

1. Saint Jerome translated the Scriptures into Latin so that more people could read and understand them. In this reading, how does he express his desire that people read the Scriptures?

2. Explain what Saint Jerome means when he says, "For the law is spiritual, and in order to understand it we need the veil to be removed and the glory of God to be seen with an uncovered face." How does the story of the eunuch relate to this statement?

3. Saint Jerome states, "You cannot advance in the Holy Scriptures unless you have an experienced guide to show you the way." Whom do you look to for guidance in the study of the Scriptures? Why?

9 Meaning Below the Surface: Faith and Science and the Literary Character of the Scriptures

Introduction

Because God's wisdom has inexplicable depths, the full meaning of a biblical text often lies beneath its surface. The variety of **literary genres** we find in the Scriptures demonstrates these depths: poems, songs, genealogies, narratives, origin accounts, miracle accounts, parables, apocalyptic sayings, and many other types of literature. Several of these types do not lend themselves to a surface-level meaning. For instance, God did not actually lift up the Israelites from slavery on a giant eagle's wings, as Exodus, chapter 15, implies. That image provides merely one way to understand the heights of liberty to which God delivered the Israelites in their escape from Egypt.

The reading in this chapter, which comes from the *United States Catholic Catechism for Adults,* first examines an important aspect of the Scriptures: its literary character. When God chose to reveal himself in human language, he inspired the authors of the Scriptures to write down the oral tradition of their cultures, using many of the ways in which humans tell stories and pass on information. As a result, the Bible reveals the consistent truth about God, but it communicates this truth in diverse literary forms.

This reading also addresses the related topic of faith and science, and particularly the Catholic understanding that the two do not stand in opposition to each other. When the Scriptures are interpreted without a sense of the deeper truth that

> **literary genres** Specific types of literature, such as poetry, narrative, creation story, parable, and so on.

God is communicating, an apparent conflict can arise between the Scriptures and human scientific understanding. By learning about the literary aspects of the Bible and the foundational truths found there, we can clearly see that faith and science do not stand against each other. Rather, both are gifts from God that help us know him better.

An example of the literary aspect of the Bible and the difficulty a literal interpretation can present can be seen in the creation accounts of Genesis, chapters 1–2. Both chapters tell the story of Creation. A creation account is its own genre; creation accounts are found in many cultures, often using symbolic language rather than historical facts. Note that it is not possible for the Genesis creation accounts to have been recorded as witnessed historical facts, because much of both accounts occurs outside human experience.

In Genesis, chapter 1, everything is created in a particular order in a perfect six days. All creation is declared "good," and humanity—created male and female—is the pinnacle of creation, made in God's glory. In chapter 2, Creation occurs in no set period of time; Adam is made first from the dirt, then the animals arrive, and finally Eve is created. Both accounts convey fundamental aspects of theological truth. God is transcendent and all-powerful, as in chapter 1; but he is also present with his creation, as in chapter 2. Humans originate from and bear God's glorious image, but we also have intrinsic needs, which include the need for companionship.

These two Creation accounts, which likely come from two different oral traditions, together convey the truth concerning God's transcendence in power and closeness in love, along with humanity's future glory and present condition of frailty. The accounts are better able to show this truth than a factual explanation of the earth's origins would be. For this reason there need not be any distinction between faith and science. The Scriptures, in terms of faith and morals, reveal truth to humanity and as a result cannot disagree with scientific studies.

The reading below from the *United States Catholic Catechism for Adults* reminds us that "the Bible is not a scientific textbook and should never be read as such; rather it reveals what God wants us to know for the sake of our salvation" (p. 61).

Excerpts from the *United States Catholic Catechism for Adults*

By the United States Conference of Catholic Bishops

Sacred Scripture

Sacred Scripture is inspired by God and is the Word of God. Therefore, God is the author of Sacred Scripture, which means he inspired the human authors, acting in and through them. Thus, God ensured that the authors taught, without error, those truths necessary for our salvation.

Inspiration is the word used for the divine assistance given to the human authors of the books of Sacred Scripture. This means that guided by the Holy Spirit, the human authors made full use of their talents and abilities while, at the same time, writing what God intended. There are many in modern society who find incredible the belief that Scripture contains the inspired word of God and so reject the Bible as a collection of stories and myths. There are others who profess belief in the Triune God and are even identified as "Scripture scholars" who work to "demythologize" the Scriptures, that is, they remove or explain away the miraculous as

The Church and Evolution

The Catholic Church has never opposed in principle the substance of Darwin's theory of evolution. In his encyclical *Humani Generis,* Pope Pius XII said that Catholics did not need to condemn the theory. Speaking to the Pontifical Academy of Sciences in 1992, John Paul II reaffirmed the Church's acceptance of evolution as a theory, so long as it does not deny God's involvement, question the validity of the human soul, or have a merely materialistic view of creation.

well as references to God's revealing words and actions. It is important to understand in the face of such challenges to Scripture that it is not simply the work of human authors as some critics allege, but truly the Word and work of God. . . .

The Visible World

In the first of two creation stories (cf. Gn 1—2:4), Scripture describes the creation of the visible world as a succession of six days of divine "work," after which God "rested" on the seventh day, the **Sabbath**. From the earliest times, Christian writers and biblical scholars have been aware that the language in the story is symbolic, for the six "days" of creation could hardly be solar days, since Genesis says that the sun was not made until the fourth day. The sequence of creation reported in Chapter 1 of the Book of Genesis is not literal or scientific, but poetic and theological. It describes a hierarchy of creatures in which human beings are the summit of visible creation. By ending the sequence of creation with the Sabbath, the story points to the adoration of God the Creator as the focal point of all the works of creation. "The heavens declare the glory of God; / the sky proclaims its builder's craft" (Ps 19:1).

The *Dogmatic Constitution on Divine Revelation* of the Second Vatican Council reminds us that "in Sacred Scripture, God speaks through human beings in human fashion," and that if we are "to ascertain what God has wished to communicate to us, [we] should carefully search out the meaning which the sacred writers really had in mind" (DV, no. 12). It goes on to say, "In determining the intention of the sacred writers, attention must be paid, inter alia [among other things], to literary forms." Chapters 1 and 2 of Genesis use symbolic language to convey fundamental truths about God and ourselves. . . .

Sabbath In the Old Testament, the "seventh day," on which God rested after completing the work of Creation. In the Old Law, the weekly day of rest to remember God's work through private prayer and communal worship. For Catholics the Sabbath is Sunday, the day on which Jesus was raised, which we are to observe with participation in the Eucharist in fulfillment of the Third Commandment.

Through the stories of creation in Chapters 1 and 2 of Genesis, God reveals himself as the Creator of all that exists, showing particularly a tender love for the high point of his creation, man and woman. The majesty and wisdom of God's creation are celebrated in the eloquence of the prophets, the lyricism of the Psalms, and the Wisdom writings of the Old Testament. Through his Incarnation, death, and Resurrection, Jesus Christ renews all creation, making it his own and filling it with the Holy Spirit.

Divine Providence

God guides his creation toward its completion or perfection through what we call his *Divine Providence*. This means that God has absolute sovereignty over all that he has made and guides his creation according to the divine plan of his will. At the same time, both the evidence of the world that we discover by our human endeavors and the testimony of Sacred Scripture show that for the unfolding of his plan, God uses secondary causes, including the laws of physics, chemistry, and biology, as well as the cooperation of our own human intellect and will. The Father of all continues to work with his Son, who is eternal Wisdom, and with the Holy Spirit, who is the inexhaustible source of life, to guide creation and humanity to the fullness of God's truth, goodness, and beauty. . . .

Issues of Faith and Science

Catholic philosophy and theology have traditionally held that the human intellect comes to know the truth through scientific discovery and philosophical reasoning and can even come to a knowledge of God and many of his purposes through an understanding of created realities.

The *Pastoral Constitution on the Church in the Modern World* (*Gaudium et Spes;* GS) of the Second Vatican Council teaches that "methodical research in all branches of knowledge, provided it is carried out in a truly scientific manner and does not override moral laws, can never conflict with the faith, because the things of the world and the things of faith derive from the same God. The humble and persevering investigator of the secrets of nature is being led, as it were, by the hand of God in spite of himself, for it is God, the conserver of all things, who made them what they are" (CCC, no. 159, citing GS, no. 36).

This does not mean that there have not been conflicts between science and religion. For example, in the seventeenth century, Galileo, building on previous discoveries, held firmly to the conviction that the earth moves around the sun. This was not acceptable to many of his contemporaries including Church authorities. As a result, he was subjected to a Church investigation and placed under house arrest for the rest of his life. Pope John Paul II ordered a study of Galileo's case, which resulted in his exoneration in 1992.

In modern times, the scientific teaching of evolution has also led to conflict with some Christians. Since 1925, the celebrated "Scopes monkey trial" in Dayton, Tennessee, has had a lasting effect on the popular understanding about evolution. The famous orator and frequent presidential candidate William Jennings Bryan argued from the principles of a literalist interpretation of the Bible. Clarence Darrow, his agnostic counterpart, ridiculed his approach as contrary to scientific progress. Through subsequent dramatic presentations like *Inherit the Wind,* on stage and in film, this debate fixed in the American mind the mistaken notion that in the debate over evolution, the only choice is between biblical literalism and Darwinism, when, in fact, there are some who recognize physical and biological evolution as the work of the divine Creator.

The Catholic Church, however, has continued to uphold the principle that there is no intrinsic conflict between science and religion. In his 1950 encyclical *Concerning Some False Opinions Threatening to Undermine the Foundations of Catholic Doctrine (Humani Generis),* Pope Pius XII applied this principle to the controversial theories of evolution, which have often been used in a materialistic or agnostic sense to argue against any divine intervention in the work of creation: "The [Magisterium] of the Church does not forbid that, in conformity with the present state of human sciences and sacred theology, research and discussions, on the part of [people] experienced in both fields, take place with regard to the doctrine of evolution, in as far as it inquires into the origin of the human body as

> " *The Catholic Church, however, has continued to uphold the principle that there is no intrinsic conflict between science and religion.* "

coming from pre-existent and living matter" (no. 36). At the same time, Pope Pius XII reiterated the doctrine that each human soul is immortal and individually created by God.

Pope John Paul II made a further commentary on this question in his 1996 Message to the Pontifical Academy of Sciences. While acknowledging the scientific evidence in favor of evolution, he cautioned that the theories of evolution that consider the human soul the seat of the intellect and will by which the human person comes to know and love God "as emerging from forces of living matter" would not be compatible with the truth about the dignity of the human person as taught in Revelation. This position does not conflict with the nature of scientific methodology in the various fields, since their method is one of observation and correlation. The spiritual dimension of the human person is of a different order that is related to yet transcends the material world and that is not reducible simply to the physical aspects of our being, which can be more readily studied by the scientific method.

For Reflection

1. According to the Second Vatican Council, quoted in the reading, why is it important for us to study and understand the different literary forms that appear in the Bible?

2. What does the reading mean when it discusses the need for "an understanding of created realities"? What is a "created reality"?

3. Based on this reading, explain the statement that "there is no intrinsic conflict between science and religion." Why is this so?

10 Scripture: God Reveals Himself through the Words of Inspired Human Preachers and Writers

Introduction

In chapter 2 you read a portion of the Second Vatican Council's document *Dogmatic Constitution on Divine Revelation (Dei Verbum)* that addresses the question of how we can know God. In this chapter we look at another section of the document. It examines the transmission of Revelation and the Scriptures in the life of the Church. The selection begins by explaining the union of Sacred Tradition and Sacred Scripture. Tradition is a living entity, fully manifested in the person of Christ and passed down in his teachings to the Apostles. This apostolic Tradition guided, for example, the Church's understanding of which ancient writings should be considered part of the Scriptures.

Tradition serves to reveal God's love to the faithful and his plan for salvation. The duty of the Church, through its teaching authority, or Magisterium, is to teach the faithful so they might contemplate the transmitted Tradition and the whole of the Scriptures "and may be filled with all the fullness of God" (Ephesians 3:19). Scripture and Tradition are innately connected and communicate with each other. Together they make up a single Deposit of the Word of God. The Church then guards and interprets this deposit.

The Scriptures, along with Tradition, play an important role in the formation of the faithful and the life of the Church. Contemplating the Scriptures during Mass prepares the faithful to examine their conscience and to partake in Christ's Body in the Eucharist.

It also aids in their prayerful worship, both in the liturgy and in their personal prayer. For this reason, the Scriptures must be made available to the faithful so they can deepen their relationship with God through reverence of and the study of the Word. The Church is required to set forward authoritative translations and to interpret the Word in writing and preaching to form a proper understanding of God's plan revealed in the Scriptures. Scripture study, when incorporated with prayer, becomes a rich and rewarding dialogue between God and the believer.

Excerpts from *Dogmatic Constitution on Divine Revelation (Dei Verbum)*
By the Second Vatican Council

HANDING ON DIVINE REVELATION

7. In His gracious goodness, God has seen to it that what He had revealed for the salvation of all nations would abide perpetually in its full integrity and be handed on to all generations. Therefore Christ the Lord, in whom the full revelation of the supreme God is brought to completion (see Cor. 1:20; 3:13; 4:6), commissioned the Apostles to preach to all men that Gospel which is the source of all saving truth and moral teaching, and to impart to them heavenly gifts. This Gospel had been promised in former times through the prophets, and Christ Himself had fulfilled it and **promulgated** it with His lips. This commission was faithfully fulfilled by the Apostles who, by their oral preaching, by example, and by observances handed on what they had received from the lips of Christ, from living with Him, and from what He did, or what they had learned through the prompting of the Holy Spirit. The commission was fulfilled, too, by those Apostles and apostolic men who under the inspiration of the same Holy Spirit committed the message of salvation to writing.

But in order to keep the Gospel forever whole

promulgate To make a teaching or writing official and authoritative.

and alive within the Church, the Apostles left bishops as their successors, "handing over" to them "the authority to teach in their own place." This Sacred Tradition, therefore, and Sacred Scripture of both the Old and New Testaments are like a mirror in which the pilgrim Church on earth looks at God, from whom she has received everything, until she is brought finally to see Him as He is, face to face (see 1 John 3:2).

8. And so the apostolic preaching, which is expressed in a special way in the inspired books, was to be preserved by an unending succession of preachers until the end of time. Therefore the Apostles, handing on what they themselves had received, warn the faithful to hold fast to the traditions which they have learned either by word of mouth or by letter (see 2 Thess. 2:15), and to fight in defense of the faith handed on once and for all (see Jude 1:3). Now what was handed on by the Apostles includes everything which contributes toward the holiness of life and increase in faith of the peoples of God; and so the Church, in her teaching, life and worship, perpetuates and hands on to all generations all that she herself is, all that she believes.

This tradition which comes from the Apostles develops in the Church with the help of the Holy Spirit. For there is a growth in the understanding of the realities and the words which have been handed down. This happens through the contemplation and study made by believers, who treasure these things in their hearts (see Luke 2:19, 51) through a penetrating understanding of the spiritual realities which they experience, and through the preaching of those who have received through Episcopal succession the sure gift of truth. For as the centuries succeed one another, the Church constantly moves forward toward the fullness of divine truth until the words of God reach their complete fulfillment in her.

The words of the holy fathers witness to the presence of this living tradition, whose wealth is poured into the practice and life of the believing and praying Church. Through the same tradition the Church's full **canon** of the sacred books is known, and the sacred writings themselves are more pro-

canon From the Greek *kanon,* meaning "standard" or "measure." A list of books that is considered to be inspired and authoritative Scripture.

foundly understood and unceasingly made active in her; and thus God, who spoke of old, uninterruptedly converses with the bride of His beloved Son; and the Holy Spirit, through whom the living voice of the Gospel resounds in the Church, and through her, in the world, leads unto all truth those who believe and makes the word of Christ dwell abundantly in them (see Col. 3:16).

9. Hence there exists a close connection and communication between sacred tradition and Sacred Scripture. For both of them, flow-

> ### The Magisterium and the Scriptures
>
> The Magisterium has a duty to interpret the Deposit of Faith, made up of Sacred Scripture and Sacred Tradition. In this sense the Magisterium acts to provide authoritative translations that accurately present God's plan and to offer aids to study God's Word. The bishops are to interpret the Scriptures in the light of the apostolic Tradition.

ing from the same divine wellspring, in a certain way merge into a unity and tend toward the same end. For Sacred Scripture is the word of God inasmuch as it is consigned to writing under the inspiration of the divine Spirit, while sacred tradition takes the word of God entrusted by Christ the Lord and the Holy Spirit to the Apostles, and hands it on to their successors in its full purity, so that led by the light of the Spirit of truth, they may in proclaiming it preserve this word of God faithfully, explain it, and make it more widely known. Consequently it is not from Sacred Scripture alone that the Church draws her certainty about everything which has been revealed. Therefore both sacred tradition and Sacred Scripture are to be accepted and venerated with the same sense of loyalty and reverence.

10. Sacred tradition and Sacred Scripture form one sacred deposit of the word of God, committed to the Church. Holding fast to this deposit the entire holy people united with their shepherds remain always steadfast in the teaching of the Apostles, in the common life, in the breaking of the bread and

> 66 *Sacred tradition and Sacred Scripture form one sacred deposit of the word of God.* 99

in prayers (see Acts 2, 42, Greek text), so that holding to, practicing and professing the heritage of the faith, it becomes on the part of the bishops and faithful a single common effort.

But the task of authentically interpreting the word of God, whether written or handed on, has been entrusted exclusively to the living teaching office of the Church, whose authority is exercised in the name of Jesus Christ. This teaching office is not above the word of God, but serves it, teaching only what has been handed on, listening to it devoutly, guarding it scrupulously and explaining it faithfully in accord with a divine commission and with the help of the Holy Spirit, it draws from this one deposit of faith everything which it presents for belief as divinely revealed.

It is clear, therefore, that sacred tradition, Sacred Scripture and the teaching authority of the Church, in accord with God's most wise design, are so linked and joined together that one cannot stand without the others, and that all together and each in its own way under the action of the one Holy Spirit contribute effectively to the salvation of souls. . . .

21. The Church has always venerated the divine Scriptures just as she venerates the body of the Lord, since, especially in the sacred liturgy, she unceasingly receives and offers to the faithful the bread of life from the table both of God's word and of Christ's body. She has always maintained them, and continues to do so, together with sacred tradition, as the supreme rule of faith, since, as inspired by God and committed once and for all to writing, they impart the word of God Himself without change, and make the voice of the Holy Spirit resound in the words of the prophets and Apostles. Therefore, like the Christian religion itself, all the preaching of the Church must be nourished and regulated by Sacred Scripture. For in the sacred books, the Father who is in heaven meets His children with great love and speaks with them; and the force and power in the word of God is so great that it stands as the support and energy of the Church, the strength of faith for her sons, the food of the soul, the pure and everlasting source of spiritual life. Consequently these words are perfectly applicable to Sacred Scripture: "For the word of God is living and active" (Heb. 4:12) and "it has power to build you up and give you your heritage among all those who are sanctified" (Acts 20:32; see 1 Thess. 2:13).

22. Easy access to Sacred Scripture should be provided for all the Christian faithful. That is why the Church from the very beginning accepted as her own that very ancient Greek translation; of the Old Testament which is called the septuagint; and she has always given a place of honor to other Eastern translations and Latin ones especially the Latin translation known as the vulgate. But since the word of God should be accessible at all times, the Church by her authority and with maternal concern sees to it that suitable and correct translations are made into different languages, especially from the original texts of the sacred books. And should the opportunity arise and the Church authorities approve, if these translations are produced in cooperation with the separated brethren as well, all Christians will be able to use them.

23. The bride of the incarnate Word, the Church taught by the Holy Spirit, is concerned to move ahead toward a deeper understanding of the Sacred Scriptures so that she may increasingly feed her sons with the divine words. Therefore, she also encourages the study of the holy Fathers of both East and West and of sacred liturgies. Catholic **exegetes** then and other students of sacred theology, working diligently together and using appropriate means, should devote their energies, under the watchful care of the sacred teaching office of the Church, to an exploration and exposition of the divine writings. This should be so done that as many ministers of the divine word as possible will be able effectively to provide the nourishment of the Scriptures for the people of God, to enlighten their minds, strengthen their wills, and set men's hearts on fire with the love of God. The sacred synod encourages the sons of the Church and Biblical scholars to continue energetically, following the mind of the Church, with the work they have so well begun, with a constant renewal of vigor.

exegetes Those who engage in the critical interpretation and explanation of a biblical text. Exegesis is a drawing out of meaning from a text, rather than forcing one's own meaning onto the text.

For Reflection

1. How did Sacred Tradition develop in the early Christian Church?

2. Explain the "close connection and communication between sacred tradition and Sacred Scripture" as presented in the reading. Why does the Church venerate both Tradition and Scripture?

3. Review *Divine Revelation*, sections 21–23. What examples do the passages give of how the Church venerates Sacred Scripture? What do the passages say about how Sacred Scripture nourishes the Church?

11 Praying the Word of God: *Lectio Divina*

Introduction

Many people struggle with prayer, because they do not know what to say when they pray. When we struggle with prayer, one place we can turn to is the Scriptures. The Church continually calls us to turn to the Scriptures in prayer so the Word of God can speak to our lives and touch our hearts. One ancient form of prayer that relies on the Scriptures and that is still popular today is *lectio divina* (a Latin phrase that literally means "divine reading"). This practice involves reflecting on the words of the Scriptures, allowing the words in the text to inspire deeper prayer and foster consistency in our relationship with God. The first step of *lectio divina* involves reading a Scripture passage aloud. This important step is often lost to modern readers. Scripture was written to be proclaimed aloud for an audience, so this primary step gives the modern reader a means to engage with the text and brings us closer to its original form and intention. Also, because readers today rarely read aloud, hearing the text may alert us to words in the text that are similar to those found in other Scripture passages, a connection that may not be as apparent when we read the Scriptures silently.

The second step in *lectio divina,* meditation, is a prayerful reflection on the text. This step means dedicating time in silence to reflect on the reading, or it means we reflect on the reading throughout the day. Once we have read aloud and meditated on the Scriptures, then in the third step, we pray over these reflections and listen carefully in return.

The fourth element, contemplation, is the consummation of the previous three steps in a deep, internal movement toward God. This often wordless aspect of prayer builds on the imaginative reflection that began while reading aloud and meditating. In this step a young student who may be sitting quietly outdoors or at home praying over Mark 4:35–40, which recounts Jesus' calming of the storm at sea, might see herself in the boat on the stormy sea with the disciples and feel the powerful peace that Christ brings in the midst of apparent chaos. Or a father, praying over Matthew 2:13–15, which recounts the angel of the Lord appearing to Joseph and instructing him to take Mary and the infant Jesus to Egypt for their safety, might imagine himself as Joseph caring for Jesus and then, while holding his newborn child, experience an inexpressible understanding of the mystery of the Incarnation.

The reading for this chapter is taken from *The Brazos Introduction to Christian Spirituality* and provides an overview of the historical development of *lectio divina,* as well as explaining each step in the practice. This method of reading and prayer is relevant today because regular practice can provide an excellent starting point for developing a prayer life because its substance is based not solely on the words of the person praying but also, and especially, on the glorious Word of the one who is sought. The Word that inspired the Scriptures is now able to speak within the believer's heart to form him or her—mind, body, and spirit—to be better able to understand God's will.

Excerpt from *The Brazos Introduction to Christian Spirituality*

By Evan Howard

Historical Portrait: An Introduction to *Lectio Divina*

Lectio Divina, a very old means of bridging scripture and spirituality, is seeing something of a revival these days. The term *lectio divina* literally means "divine reading." It was used to refer to the material read as well as to the act of reading holy

> " *The term* lectio divina *literally means "divine reading."* "

books. John Cassian (c. 360–430), who visited the deserts of the East and carried their wisdom to the Western monasteries, refers to the practice in his works. It is Saint Benedict (the patriarch of western monasticism, c. 480–550), however, who explicitly encourages the practice, making it a standard part of monastic life for centuries to follow. In his *Rule,* or guide for monastic living, Benedict instructs that "the brothers should have specified times for manual labor as well as for prayerful reading (*lectio divina*)."[1]

The practice of prayerful reading developed within the context of Western monastic life, in a somewhat predictable schedule of prayer, work, and reading. The times of prayer (known as the Divine Office) were dominated by common worship gatherings, where psalms and scriptures are chanted, intercessions are made, times of silence are kept, and faith is affirmed. Times of work involved diligent, but not frantic, activity. Times of reading, of *lectio,* enabled one to bring it all together. Reading, study, imagination, prayer, reflection, and silence were all combined in *lectio.* As Jean Leclercq writes, "*Lectio* provided calm and relaxed meditation, a loving disposition, and a fervent interest in exegesis or at least in its results. It created a spiritual atmosphere within which the problems dealt with by biblical silence remained religious problems—an atmosphere of faith in which one learned, in a manner always mysterious, to enter into the experience of the inspired authors, and especially of Christ."[2]

While *lectio divina* developed as a single, integrative practice, it tends to be discussed in terms of four separate elements. The first element of *lectio divina* is simply reading *(lectio).* In the early monastic culture, reading was usually done out loud, with the consequence that a reading was also a hearing of the text. In oral reading, already the mouth, the

---

Christian Prayer

Our relationship with God is based on communication. God communicates with us through Revelation in the world and in the Scriptures. We respond through prayer and worship. The Scriptures give us many examples of prayers: lamentations, songs of joy, thanksgiving, requests, and pleas for help. Regardless of the style or words used, an open heart and sincere love for God are all that are required for meaningful prayer.

ears, and the mind are involved in the internalization of the passage. Slow reading naturally shades into the second element: meditation *(meditatio)*. The root idea of scriptural meditation is still that of a wholehearted, prayerful reflection on the text, making use of mind, feelings, imagination, and intention. The third element of *lectio divina* is that of prayer *(oratio)*. The prayer of *lectio* expresses the sincere movement of the heart to God, stimulated by the reading of and meditation on scripture. In reading God offers himself to us. In prayer we offer ourselves to God. The final element of *lectio divina* is contemplation *(contemplatio)*. Contemplation points "to those moments in prayer when some form of more direct contact with God is attained."[3]

Whether our approach to prayerful reading employs well-defined techniques for interacting with the text or whether we simply sit down and relax with our Bible, present with God as we read, *lectio divina* can be a helpful means of integrating biblical studies and Christian spirituality. A number of introductions to the practice are available today. *Lectio divina* is one monastic practice that is as relevant today as it was in the fifth century.

Endnotes

1. *The Rules of Benedict,* trans. Anthony C. Meisel and M. L. del Mastro (New York: Image Doubleday, 1975), 48.1.
2. Jean Leclercq, "Prayer and Contemplation: II. Western," in *Christian Spirituality: Origins to the Twelfth Century,* ed. Bernard McGinn, John Meyendorff, and Jean Leclercq, vol. 16, World Spirituality: An Encyclopedic History of the Religious Quest (New York: Crossroad, 1985), 420.
3. Bernard McGinn, *The Growth of Mysticism: Gregory the Great through the 12th Century,* vol. 2, The Presence of God: A History of Western Christian Mysticism (New York: Crossroad, 1994), 139.

For Reflection

1. What are some key differences between the similar steps of meditating, praying, and contemplating in the *lectio divina* process as described in this reading?

2. How does the practice of *lectio divina* promote a "loving disposition," as Jean Leclercq says?

3. Look at these texts: Mark 4:35–41, John 21:15–17, and Romans 8:5–14. Use one of them to engage in the four-step practice of *lectio divina* described here: read aloud, meditate, pray, and contemplate. What ideas come to mind? What do you hear when you listen? What new understanding do you find in the text?

Part 3
Understanding Scripture

12 Diplomacy and Scripture: Pope Pius XII Navigates Catholic Biblical Scholarship into the Modern Era

Introduction

Eugenio Pacelli, son of a prominent Italian lawyer, was born in 1876. After being ordained a priest, he worked in the Vatican's secretary of state office for sixteen years. He was ordained bishop and named **apostolic nuncio** to Bavaria (a province in the German Empire) in 1917 and to the country of Germany in 1920. During this time he played a part in helping to persuade Germany to accept the peace agreement that ended World War I. He was elected Pope in 1939, becoming Pius XII, just as World War II was beginning. Through diplomatic means Pius attempted to prevent escalation of the war. After realizing this was futile, he sought to make neutrality the appropriate strategy to be followed by the Vatican.

Pius was a successful negotiator, and his diplomatic skills were prominent in his governance of the Church. His forty encyclicals encouraged reforms in many aspects of the Church, including liturgy and biblical studies. One of his most influential encyclicals was *Divino Afflante Spiritu,* which sought to moderate traditional Catholic methods of biblical interpretation with more modern scholarly perspectives.

The midtwentieth century saw a great deal of growth and change in methods of interpreting the Scriptures. These modern perspectives emphasized

apostolic nuncio A diplomat who acts as an ambassador between the Vatican and another nation.

the historical context and language of the human biblical authors and the literary forms found in the text rather than a strictly literal interpretation. Pius, being a diplomat, sought to moderate the Catholic position on interpreting the Scriptures. His reforms not only updated Catholic scholarship with modern methods but also reconnected them to the early Fathers of the Church, who emphasized understanding the historical sense of the text as an essential first step to interpretation.

Divino Afflante Spiritu was monumental for its time. It called for biblical translations to be based on the original languages of Hebrew and Greek, at a time when all Catholic bibles and the Mass readings were translated from the Latin Vulgate. The document also emphasized the importance of evaluating the literary form of the text in the interpretation. Poetry needs to be interpreted as poetry; a letter needs to be interpreted in a different way, as does a creation account, and so forth. Exegetes could appreciate the literary diversity and richness found in the canon and use this data to interpret the texts. Pius's encyclical has maintained considerable influence. It is frequently cited in the Vatican Council II declaration *Dogmatic Constitution on Divine Revelation (Dei Verbum),* the Pontifical Biblical Commission's 1993 document *Interpretation of the Bible in the Church,* and the present works of Pope Benedict XVI.

Excerpt from *Divino Afflante Spiritu*

By Pope Pius XII

11. There is no one who cannot easily perceive that the conditions of biblical studies and their subsidiary sciences have greatly changed within the last fifty years. For, apart from anything else, when Our Predecessor published the Encyclical Letter **Providentissimus Deus,** hardly a single place in Palestine had begun to

Providentissimus Deus An encyclical issued in 1893 by Pope Leo XIII on the study of Holy Scriptures.

be explored by means of relevant excavations. Now, however, this kind of investigation is much more frequent and, since more precise methods and technical skill have been developed in the course of actual experience, it gives us information at once more abundant and more accurate. How much light has been derived from these explorations for the more correct and fuller understanding of the Sacred Books all experts know, as well as all those who devote themselves to these studies. The value of these excavations is enhanced by the discovery from time to time of written documents, which help much towards the knowledge of the languages, letters, events, customs, and forms of worship of most ancient times. And of no less importance is **papyri** which have contributed so much to the knowledge of the discovery and investigation, so frequent in our times, of letters and institutions, both public and private, especially of the time of Our Savior.

12. Moreover ancient codices of the Sacred Books have been found and edited with discerning thoroughness; the exegesis of the Fathers of the Church has been more widely and thoroughly examined; in fine the manner of speaking, relating and writing in use among the ancients is made clear by innumerable examples. All these advantages which, not without a special design of Divine Providence, our age has acquired, are as it were an invitation and inducement to interpreters of the Sacred Literature to make diligent use of this light, so abundantly given, to penetrate more deeply, explain more clearly and expound more lucidly the Divine Oracles. If, with the greatest satisfaction of mind, We perceive that these same interpreters have resolutely answered and still continue to answer this call, this is certainly not the last or least of the fruits of the Encyclical Letter *Providentissimus Deus,* by which Our Predecessor Leo XIII, foreseeing as it were this new development of biblical studies, summoned Catholic exegetes to labor and wisely defined the direction and the method to be followed in that labor. . . .

37. Nevertheless no one, who has a correct idea of biblical inspiration, will be surprised to find, even in the Sacred Writers, as in other ancient authors, certain fixed ways of

papyri Ancient scrolls and pages made from papyrus plants.

expounding and narrating, certain definite idioms, especially of a kind peculiar to the Semitic tongues, so-called approximations, and certain hyperbolical modes of expression, nay, at times, even paradoxical, which even help to impress the ideas more deeply on the mind. For of the modes of expression which, among ancient peoples, and especially those of the East, human language used to express its thought, none is excluded from the Sacred Books, provided the way of speaking adopted in no wise contradicts the holiness and truth of God, as, with his customary wisdom, the Angelic Doctor already observed in these words: "In Scripture divine things are presented to us in the manner which is in common use amongst men." For as the substantial Word of God became like to men in all things, "except sin," so the words of God, expressed in human language, are made like to human speech in every respect, except error. In this consists that "condescension" of the God of providence, which St. John Chrysostom extolled with the highest praise and repeatedly declared to be found in the Sacred Books.

> **Figures of Speech in Biblical Languages**
>
> Cultures tend to have different forms of expression that are not literal but rather convey a figurative meaning. For instance, in our own culture, we say, "It's raining cats and dogs," but we mean only that it's raining heavily, not that animals are falling from the sky. The biblical authors had several such figures of speech, typical of the cultures and times in which they lived. For example, 2 Samuel 3:9 reads, "May God do thus and so to Abner." For modern readers the phrase *do thus and so* might be confusing, but people reading or hearing this in ancient Israel would know the phrase means to punish or treat poorly.

38. Hence the Catholic commentator, in order to comply with the present needs of biblical studies, in explaining the Sacred Scripture and in demonstrating and proving its immunity from all error, should also make a

> *. . . so the words of God, expressed in human language, are made like to human speech in every respect, except error.*

prudent use of this means, determine, that is, to what extent the manner of expression or the literary mode adopted by the sacred writer may lead to a correct and genuine interpretation; and let him be convinced that this part of his office cannot be neglected without serious detriment to Catholic exegesis. Not infrequently—to mention only one instance—when some persons reproachfully charge the Sacred Writers with some historical error or inaccuracy in the recording of facts, on closer examination it turns out to be nothing else than those customary modes of expression and narration peculiar to the ancients, which used to be employed in the mutual dealings of social life and which in fact were sanctioned by common usage.

For Reflection

1. What reasons does Pope Pius XII give for moderating Catholic biblical studies with modern methods?

2. In light of earlier readings, explain what Pius means when he states, "so the words of God, expressed in human language, are made like to human speech in every respect, except error."

3. The biblical authors used many types of literature and forms of speech to express their relationship with God. Keeping these different literary types in mind, how can study of the Scriptures deepen your understanding of God's Word?

13 Moderation for Interpretation

Introduction

Previously in this book, you read that all are born with a longing for God and that we can find him revealed in Scripture and Tradition. At the same time, the Church reminds us that proper interpretation of the Scriptures requires careful study and attention to details surrounding the text. These details include the historical and cultural context of the author, the literary genre of the text, and the interpretation of that text within the Tradition and authority of the Church.

This chapter presents an excerpt from the *United States Catholic Catechism for Adults* that teaches an appropriate means of interpreting the Scriptures based on moderation and attention to the literary and historical aspects of the text. By promoting moderation, the Adult Catechism seeks to warn against the practices of biblical literalism and biblical reductionism. Biblical literalism bases interpretation on the literal meaning of the Bible's words without regard to the historical setting in which the writings or teachings were first developed. Biblical reductionism entirely disregards the divine aspect of the Scriptures, simply viewing them as literary and historical texts.

The Church reminds us that the Scriptures are the Word of God communicated through human authors and their means of expression. This includes a variety of literary forms and figures of speech, as we have seen. Yet the Scriptures are not to be seen as simply symbolic. The Scriptures proclaim God's direct intervention in human history; the importance of this message cannot be diminished, because it is a central facet of Revelation as a whole. From this standpoint, Catholic biblical interpretation seeks to attain a moderate position between literalism and reductionism to help us appreciate both the spiritual and historical qualities that the Spirit and human authors apply within the text.

Excerpt from the *United States Catholic Catechism for Adults*

By the United States Conference of Catholic Bishops

Interpretation of Scripture

When interpreting Scripture, we should be attentive to what God wanted to reveal through the authors for our salvation. We need to see Scriptures as a unified whole with Jesus Christ at the center. We must also read Scripture within the living Tradition of the whole Church, so that we may come to grasp a true interpretation of the Scriptures. The task of giving an authoritative interpretation of the Word of God has been entrusted to the Magisterium. Last, we need to remember and recognize that there is a coherence of the truths of faith within Scripture (cf. CCC, nos. 112–114).

The Church recognizes two **senses of Scripture,** the **literal** and the **spiritual.** In probing the literal meaning of the texts, it is necessary to determine their literary form, such as history, hymns, wisdom sayings, poetry, parable, or other forms of figurative language. "The *literal sense* is the meaning conveyed by the words of Scripture and discovered by exegesis [the process scholars use to determine the meaning of the text], following the rules of sound interpretation: 'All other senses of Sacred Scripture are based on the literal'" (CCC, no. 116, citing St. Thomas Aquinas, *Summa Theologiae* I, 1, 10).

senses of Scripture The different levels of meaning that may be discerned through study of the text.

literal sense A form of biblical interpretation that considers the explicit meaning of the text. It lays the foundation for all other senses of the Scriptures.

spiritual sense A form of biblical interpretation that goes beyond the literal sense to consider what the narratives and events of the Scriptures signify and mean for salvation.

The spiritual senses of Sacred Scripture derive from the unity of God's plan of salvation. The text of Scripture discloses God's plan. The realities and events of which it speaks can also be signs of the divine plan. . . .

The Church's Scripture scholars are expected to work according to these principles to develop a better understanding of Scripture for God's people. Interpretation of Scripture is ultimately subject to the judgment of the Magisterium, which exercises the divine commission to hold fast to and to interpret authoritatively God's Word.

Other Biblical Interpretations

Our response to God's call to holiness involves regular, prayerful study of Scripture. "Such is the force and power of the Word of God that it can serve . . . the children of the Church as strength for their faith, food for the soul, and a pure and lasting font of spiritual life" (CCC, no. 131, citing DV, no. 21).

Catholic biblical scholars have made distinguished contributions to scriptural studies. Their outstanding service to the Church has assisted believers to grow in their faith by an authentic understanding of Scripture. Two of the various challenges they face come from interpretations posed, on the one hand, by those who interpret the Bible only in a literal fashion, and, on the other hand, by those who deny the supernatural aspects of the Gospels.

The Book of Revelation in Catholic Perspective

The Book of Revelation is one of the most misunderstood books of the Bible. It has commonly been interpreted today to be either entirely future-oriented or only symbolic. Catholic biblical scholars view the book as reflecting the historical situation of its author and audience, which includes the violent persecution of Christians under the Emperor Domitian (ca. AD 90). The vibrant and violent imagery found in the book is informed by Jewish apocalyptic texts both inside and outside the canon, as well as the materialistic and power-oriented culture of the Roman Empire. The book uses the image of Christ as a slaughtered lamb to convey the truth that God's sacrificial love is more powerful than human corruption and greed. The book conveys the truth of a future judgment and God's direct intervention to reclaim and renew his creation within his divine plan.

Biblical Literalism

In the United States a certain number of Christians of many denominations— often called Fundamentalists—have adopted the supremacy of Scripture as their sole foundation. They also approach Scripture from a viewpoint of private interpretation. This they do in the strictest literal sense without appreciation of the various literary forms that the biblical authors used within the specific cultural circumstances in which they were writing.

The Church's response to Fundamentalism is that Revelation is transmitted by Apostolic Tradition and Scripture together. The Church and Apostolic Tradition existed before the written New Testament. Her Apostles preached the Gospel orally before writing it down. The Apostles appointed bishops to succeed them with the authority to continue their teaching. Scripture alone is insufficient. Authoritative teaching is also needed. That is given to us by the Church's teaching office. Catholics, then, accept Scripture and Tradition as one "sacred deposit of the Word of God" (CCC, no. 97, citing DV, no. 10). Although this sets us apart from those who believe only in the Bible as their source of revelation, Catholics accept and honor both Scripture and Tradition "with equal sentiments of devotion and reverence" (CCC, no. 82, citing DV, no. 9).

In response to biblical literalism, the Church holds that "the books of Scripture firmly, faithfully and without error, teach that truth which God, for the sake of our salvation, wished to see confided to the sacred Scriptures" (DV, no. 11). At the same time, the Church recognizes that the interpreter of Scripture needs to attend to the literary forms—such as poetry, symbol, parable, history, song, or prayer—in which the Bible is written. The interpreter "must look for that meaning which the sacred writer . . . given the circumstance of his time and culture, intended to express and did in fact express, through the medium of a contemporary literary form" (DV, no. 12).

Historical Reductionism

Another challenge comes from scholars and others who deny the supernatural aspects of the Gospels, such as the Incarnation, Virgin Birth, miracles, and the Resurrection. We call this *reductionism* because it reduces all Scripture to the natural order and eliminates the reality of divine intervention.

The Church's Pontifical Biblical Commission has dealt with approaches of this kind in its publications *Instruction on the Historical Truth of the Gospels* and *The Interpretation of the Bible in the Church*. The Pontifical Biblical Commission lists five unacceptable assumptions found in forms of scriptural interpretation:

> " *The Bible is more than a human work; it is God's words put into human words. It will always be a fountain of faith for those who read it in a spirit of prayer.* "

1. the denial of a supernatural order;
2. the denial of God's intervention in the world through revelation;
3. the denial of the possibility and existence of miracles;
4. the incompatibility of faith with historical truth;
5. an almost *a priori* denial of the historical value and nature of the documents of revelation. (Pontifical Biblical Commission, *Historical Truth of the Gospels* [1964], no. 5)

The Church approaches Scripture as God's revealed Word. Its authors wrote under the guidance and inspiration of the Holy Spirit. The Bible is more than a human work; it is God's words put into human words. It will always be a fountain of faith for those who read it in a spirit of prayer.

a priori From the Latin, meaning reasoning based on general principles rather than observed facts.

For Reflection

1. How do the literal and spiritual senses of the Scriptures offer a balanced approach to interpreting the Scriptures?

2. Biblical literalism often excludes the role of Tradition in interpretation. Based on the reading in this chapter, explain how Tradition influences the interpretation of the Scriptures and how this interpretation responds to literalism.

3. How does historical reductionism influence the interpretation of the Scriptures? What does this view leave out of its analysis of the text?

14 A Matter for the Whole Church: The Rules and Responsibility of Interpreting the Scriptures

Introduction

Previous chapters examined what the Second Vatican Council document *Dogmatic Constitution on Divine Revelation (Dei Verbum)* taught about God's Revelation to humanity and the nature of the Scriptures. This chapter again returns to *Divine Revelation* and explores the issue of the inspiration and interpretation of the Scriptures.

Scripture is complex in both substance and meaning. It is a human work, being written by humans using human language and literary forms, to be read by an audience of humans. Yet Scripture is mysteriously also a divine work. God is the ultimate author of the Scriptures. Through the Holy Spirit, God inspired the human writers to communicate spiritual truths, both on and beneath the surface of the text. *Divine Revelation* tells us that the books contained in the Scriptures undoubtedly teach "solidly, faithfully and without error that truth which God wanted put into sacred writings for the sake of salvation" (11).

Because the fullest meaning of the Word of God is at times found only beneath the human words of the text, we must undertake a deep exploration of the text before we can sufficiently understand the truth being conveyed. For this reason, *Divine Revelation* offers three means of studying the Scriptures. First, one should consider the historical and cultural background of the author and audience. This may provide a contextualized meaning as one begins to make sense of the text. Second, one needs always to consider the literary form, or genre, of the text. As we have read in previous chapters, a song cannot be interpreted the same way as a drama or a letter. Third, biblical texts should be read in the light of the whole of the Scriptures. Because God reveals himself gradually over time (see chapter 1), so too can aspects of truth be revealed in sequence in human history. What is said in part by one author can be restated more completely by a later author.

This reading from *Divine Revelation* provides an excellent foundation for our understanding of Sacred Scripture and Divine Inspiration. Additionally, it offers guidance for the proper interpretation of the Scriptures, so we may more fully understand the truths God conveys through it for us and his Church.

Excerpts from *Dogmatic Constitution on Divine Revelation (Dei Verbum)*
By the Second Vatican Council

Sacred Scripture, Its Inspiration and Divine Interpretation

11. Those divinely revealed realities which are contained and presented in Sacred Scripture have been committed to writing under the inspiration of the Holy Spirit. For holy mother Church, relying on the belief of the Apostles (see John 20:31; 2 Tim. 3:16; 2 Peter 1:19–20, 3:15–16), holds that the books of both the Old and New Testaments in their entirety, with all their parts, are sacred

> " Those divinely revealed realities which are contained and presented in Sacred Scripture have been committed to writing under the inspiration of the Holy Spirit. "

and canonical because written under the inspiration of the Holy Spirit, they have God as their author and have been handed on as such to the Church herself. In composing the sacred books, God chose men and while employed by Him they made use of their powers and abilities, so that with Him acting in them and through them, they, as true authors, consigned to writing everything and only those things which He wanted.

Therefore, since everything asserted by the inspired authors or sacred writers must be held to be asserted by the Holy Spirit, it follows that the books of Scripture must be acknowledged as teaching solidly, faithfully and without error that truth which God wanted put into sacred writings for the sake of salvation. Therefore "all Scripture is divinely inspired and has its use for teaching the truth and refuting error, for reformation of manners and discipline in right living, so that the man who belongs to God may be efficient and equipped for good work of every kind" (2 Tim. 3:16–17, Greek text).

12. However, since God speaks in Sacred Scripture through men in human fashion, the interpreter of Sacred Scripture, in order to see clearly what God wanted to communicate to us, should carefully investigate what meaning the sacred writers really intended, and what God wanted to manifest by means of their words.

To search out the intention of the sacred writers, attention should be given, among other things, to "literary forms." For truth is set forth and expressed differently in texts which are variously historical, prophetic, poetic, or of other forms of discourse. The interpreter must investigate what meaning the sacred writer intended to express and actually expressed in particular circumstances by using contemporary literary forms in accordance with the situation of his own time and culture. For the correct understanding of what the sacred author wanted to assert, due attention must be paid to the customary and characteristic styles of feeling, speaking and narrating which prevailed at the time of the sacred writer, and to the

The Unity of the Whole Bible

When the Bible is taken as a whole, God's revealed truth is presented without error. This is the case in many Old Testament passages, whose Christian meaning can be completely and accurately understood only in light of New Testament revelations. Take, for example, Isaiah 7:14: "Therefore the Lord himself will give you this sign: the virgin shall be with child, and bear a son, and shall name him Immanuel." The passage is fully understood in light of the birth of Jesus to the Virgin Mary.

patterns men normally employed at that period in their everyday dealings with one another.

But, since Holy Scripture must be read and interpreted in the sacred spirit in which it was written, no less serious attention must be given to the content and unity of the whole of Scripture if the meaning of the sacred texts is to be correctly worked out. The living tradition of the whole Church must be taken into account along with the harmony which exists between elements of the faith. It is the task of exegetes to work according to these rules toward a better understanding and explanation of the meaning of Sacred Scripture, so that through preparatory study the judgment of the Church may mature. For all of what has been said about the way of interpreting Scripture is subject finally to the judgment of the Church, which carries out the divine commission and ministry of guarding and interpreting the word of God.

13. In Sacred Scripture, therefore, while the truth and holiness of God always remains intact, the marvelous **"condescension"** of eternal wisdom is clearly shown, "that we may learn the gentle kindness of God, which words cannot express, and how far He has gone in adapting His language with thoughtful concern for our weak human nature." For the words of God, expressed in human language, have been made like human discourse, just as the word of the eternal Father, when He took to Himself the flesh of human weakness, was in every way made like men.

condescension In Christian theology, the nearness of God's Word, coming down from Heaven to be present with humanity.

For Reflection

1. Based on this reading, explain how the Scriptures are both human literary works and the inspired Word of God.

2. Why is it important to investigate and understand both the literary form and cultural conditions in which the Scriptures were written?

3. In your own words, explain the following: "For the words of God, expressed in human language, have been made like human discourse, just as the word of the eternal Father, when He took to Himself the flesh of human weakness, was in every way made like men."

15 The Four Senses of Scripture in the Early Church

Introduction

In the fourth century, Christianity moved from being a persecuted religion in the Roman Empire to being more accepted and eventually becoming the official state religion of the empire. Many Christians at that time worried that the spiritual quality of the Church would diminish as a result of its greater popularity. In partial response to this concern, many Christians sought to devote themselves to monastic life apart from society. Saint John Cassian (ca. 360–435) was a monk at the time of this shift from persecution to acceptance, and he wanted to offer advice and structure for those who sought God in the monastic life, away from the material wealth of the Roman Empire. His book, *The Conferences,* compiles discussions from interviews with abbots in Egypt and Europe, giving recommendations on many aspects of monastic life.

allegorical sense Relating symbolically to parallel concepts in a separate story or set of themes.

tropological sense *Tropological* comes from the Greek *tropos,* meaning "manner" or "way." This sense concerns the manner in which we are to live. Also referred to as the "moral" sense.

anagogical sense *Anagogical* comes from the Greek, meaning "upward." This sense of the Scriptures concerns what is upward in terms of the future, eternal salvation, or both.

One of Cassian's greatest contributions in this work is his explanation of the four senses of the Scriptures that are helpful for interpretation: the literal, **allegorical,** moral (also known as **tropological**), and **anagogical** senses. Although Origen (AD 185–253), Saint Jerome, Saint Augustine, and other great scholars before Cassian used these senses at times in their many works, Cassian is credited for clearly naming and defining all of them in a single work.

Cassian first identifies two categories of senses of the Scriptures: the literal and the spiritual. The literal level concerns the historical context of the author and audience and the original intention and specific details of the text. The spiritual senses presume that the human author was not necessarily aware that the Holy Spirit was working through him or her when writing, so a spiritual truth may be sought in the text, even though it is not apparent at the literal level.

As mentioned above, there are three spiritual senses: allegorical, moral, and anagogical. The allegorical sense discerns a message of faith that parallels a story in a text. For example, Origen interpreted the Parable of the Good Samaritan as an allegory telling the story of salvation history: the man who is robbed is Adam; Christ is the Good Samaritan; the Church is the inn. The allegorical sense is helpful in broadening the message of a story to teach the faithful important lessons about salvation. The moral sense searches for a moral lesson in a text. In Psalm 137, we may find it confusing that the psalmist embraces violence against children. Origen found a moral meaning: we should take our sins while they are young and beat them against the Rock of Christ. The last sense, anagogical (from the Greek, meaning "to lead upward"), concerns our final destination with God in salvation. The story of the Transfiguration, from an anagogical perspective, points to the future glory that all believers will share as part of the risen Body of Christ.

The reading from Cassian is relevant for us today for at least two reasons. First, it is the earliest and best consolidation of these four senses of the Scriptures, and as such it is an outstanding bridge to the thought and practice of the earliest Scripture scholars. Second, with the Church's renewed interest in the interpretation of the Scriptures, Cassian's explanation offers four useful and practical ways of interpreting the Scriptures that are founded on sound Tradition and also aid the modern reader. There are different types of Scripture passages—many are comforting and hopeful, but many others can seem obscure, difficult, or even frightening. Being able to recognize both the historical meaning of the author and the message of the Holy Spirit for the faithful will foster our love of sacred texts and a healthy spirituality for today's Church.

Excerpt from *The Conferences*

By John Cassian

Thus, as we said above, *practical* knowledge is distributed among many subjects and interests, but *theoretical* is divided into two parts, i.e., the historical interpretation and the spiritual sense. Whence also Solomon when he had summed up the manifold grace of the Church, added: "for all who are with her are clothed with double garments"(Proverbs 31: 21). But of spiritual knowledge there are three kinds, tropological, allegorical, anagogical, of which we read as follows in Proverbs: "But do you describe these things to yourself in three ways according to the largeness of your heart" (Proverbs 22: 20). And so the history embraces the knowledge of things past and visible, as it is repeated in this way by the Apostle: "For it is written that Abraham had two sons, the one by a bondwoman, the other by a free: but he who was

> *Thus, as we said above, practical knowledge is distributed among many subjects and interests, but theoretical is divided into two parts, i.e., the historical interpretation and the spiritual sense.*

of the bondwoman was born after the flesh, but he who was of the free was by promise." But to the allegory belongs what follows, for what actually happened is said to have prefigured the form of some mystery "For these," says he, "are the two covenants, the one from Mount Sinai, which gendereth into bondage, which is Agar. For Sinai is a mountain in Arabia, which is compared to Jerusalem which now is, and is in bondage with her children." But the anagogical sense rises from spiritual mysteries even to still more sublime and sacred secrets of heaven, and is subjoined by the Apostle in these words: "But Jerusalem which is above is free, which is the mother of us. For it is written, Rejoice, thou barren that bearest not, break forth and cry, thou that travailest not, for many are the children of the desolate more than of her that hath an husband" (Galatians 4: 22–27). The tropological sense is the moral explanation which has to do with improvement of life and practical teaching, as if we were to understand by these two covenants practical and theoretical instruction, or at any rate as if we were to want to take Jerusalem or Sion as the soul of man, according to this: "Praise the Lord, O Jerusalem: praise thy God, O Sion" (Psalm 147: 12). And so these four previously mentioned figures coalesce, if we desire, in one subject, so that one and the same Jerusalem can be taken in four senses: historically as the city of the Jews; allegorically as Church of Christ, anagogically as the heavenly city of God "which is the mother of us all," tropologically, as the soul of man, which is frequently subject to praise or blame from the Lord under this title. . . .

> **Overview of the Spiritual Senses**
>
> The allegorical sense sees the text as prefiguring or paralleling a story of salvation; the moral, or tropological, sense finds ethical guidance; and the anagogical sense focuses on future salvation. We can look at the biblical image of the Temple to see these senses. From an allegorical perspective, the Temple is Jesus: in John 2: 19–21 he says that he is the Temple that will be destroyed and raised up. In the moral sense, our body is the "temple of the Holy Spirit" (1 Corinthians 6:19). As a result we are to treat our bodies with the love and reverence owed to the dwelling place of God. Finally, the anagogical sense focuses on Heaven, where we will find our eternal home with God.

But "doctrine" unfolds the simple course of historical exposition, under which is contained no more secret sense, but what is declared by the very words: as in his passage: "For I delivered unto you first of all what I also received, how that Christ died for our sins according to the Scriptures, and that He was buried, and that He rose again on the third day, and that he was seen of Cephas;" (1 Corinthians 15: 3–5) and: "God sent His Son, made of a woman, made under the law, to redeem them that were under the law;" (Galatians 4: 4–5) or this: "Hear, O Israel, the Lord the God is one Lord" (Deuteronomy 6: 4).

For Reflection

1. After reading this chapter, what is your understanding of the literal and spiritual senses of the Scriptures?

2. Read the Parable of the Prodigal Son (see Luke 15:11–32). Review the passage using each of the spiritual senses of the Scriptures (allegorical, moral, and anagogical) as described by John Cassian. Identify examples from the parable that illustrate each sense.

3. Cassian believed studying with the literal sense and the three spiritual senses aids the believer's prayer life and devotion to the Scriptures. How can you use these four senses to enhance your own prayer life and devotion to the Scriptures?

16 The Historical Method Is Indispensable for Studying a Historical Faith

Introduction

The renowned theologian Cardinal Joseph Ratzinger was elected Pope on April 19, 2005, becoming Pope Benedict XVI. During his papacy, the majority of his writings were papal letters and speeches for the expansive audience of the church at large. However, Benedict also published works of a more scholarly nature under both his birth name and his papal title. One of these works, a book called *Jesus of Nazareth,* offers an analysis of Christ as presented in the Gospels and the Church's Tradition. In this book Benedict explains and commends the historical-critical method for the interpretation of the Scriptures. He echoes what he stated in the introduction to the Pontifical Biblical Commission's document *Interpretation of the Bible in the Church:* namely, that the historical-critical method is indispensable for studying the Scriptures.

Because Christianity believes in a God who acts and reveals himself in history, methods for studying his Word in the Scriptures must take history into account as a foundational step in understanding what is revealed in his Word. Benedict clarifies that the historical-critical method has limitations and cannot exhaust the meaning of God's inspired texts. The method's emphasis, however, on reading each book within the context of the human author's historical and cultural situation offers a clear path for us to develop the necessary insight into the human author's original intended meaning. Tracing such viewpoints can help us recognize the development and richness in the biblical tradition throughout the different books of the Scriptures.

This chapter's reading, a selection from *Jesus of Nazareth,* offers a model of interpretation of the Scriptures that is both spiritually formative and objectively grounded. It continues in the spirit of Pope Pius XII and *Dogmatic Constitution on Divine Revelation (Dei Verbum)* at Vatican Council II in helping Catholic devotion to progress in line with the Catholic intellectual tradition. This tradition has always balanced faith and reason as essential arguments to theological study. In this case faith and reason find their object in the study of the history that informs the biblical authors, so we can develop a more informed interpretation of their works.

Excerpt from *Jesus of Nazareth*
By Joseph Ratzinger / Pope Benedict XVI

I would like to sketch at least the broad outlines of the methodology, drawn from these documents, that has guided me in writing this book. The first point is that the historical-critical method—specifically because of the intrinsic nature of theology and faith—is and remains an indispensable dimension of exegetical work. For it is of the very essence of biblical faith to be about real historical events. It does not tell stories symbolizing suprahistorical truths, but is based on history, history that took place here on this earth. The *factum historicum* (historical fact) is not an interchangeable symbolic cipher for biblical faith, but the foundation on which it stands: ***Et incarnatus est***—when we say these words, we acknowledge God's actual entry into real history.

If we push this history aside, Christian faith as such disappears and is recast as some other religion. So if history, if facticity in this sense, is an essential dimension of Christian faith, then faith must expose itself to the historical method—indeed, faith itself demands this. I have already mentioned the conciliar

et incarnatus est A Latin phrase that means literally "and became flesh." It is used to refer to the Incarnation of Jesus Christ.

Constitution on Divine Revelation; it makes the same point quite explicitly in paragraph 12 and goes on to list some concrete elements of method that have to be kept in mind when interpreting Scripture. The Pontifical Biblical Commission's document on the interpretation of Holy Scripture develops the same idea much more amply in the chapter entitled "Methods and Approaches for Interpretation."

> 66 *If we push this history aside, Christian faith as such disappears and is recast as some other religion.* 99

The historical-critical method—let me repeat—is an indispensable tool, given the structure of Christian faith. But we need to add two points. This method is a fundamental dimension of exegesis, but it does not exhaust the interpretive task for someone who sees the biblical writings as a single corpus of Holy Scripture inspired by God. We will have to return to this point at greater length in a moment.

For the time being, it is important—and this is a second point—to recognize the limits of the historical-critical method itself. For someone who considers himself directly addressed by the Bible today, the method's first limit is that by its very nature it has to leave the biblical word in the past. It is a historical method, and that means that it investigates the then-current context of events in which the texts originated. It attempts to identify and to understand the past—as it was in itself—with the greatest possible precision, in order then to find out what the author could have said and intended to say in the context of the mentality and events of the time. To the extent that it remains true to itself, the historical method not only has to investigate the biblical word as a thing of the past, but also has to let it remain in the past. It can glimpse points of contact with the present and it can try to apply the biblical

The Historical-Critical Method

The historical-critical method encompasses a number of disciplines that attempt to study the context, and thus the meaning, of the biblical authors' work. These include the study of history, the social sciences, classical languages and cultures, and literature and its different genres, as well as the comparison of texts within a historical framework.

word to the present; the one thing it cannot do is make it into something present *today*—that would be overstepping its bounds. Its very precision in interpreting the reality of the past is both its strength and its limit.

This is connected with a further point. Because it is a historical method, it presupposes the uniformity of the context within which the events of history unfold. It must therefore treat the biblical words it investigates as human words. On painstaking reflection, it can intuit something of the "deeper value" the word contains. It can in some sense catch the sounds of a higher dimension through the human word, and so open up the method to self-transcendence. But its specific object is the human word as human.

Ultimately, it considers the individual books of Scripture in the context of their historical period, and then analyzes them further according to their sources. The unity of all of these writings as one "Bible," however, is not something it can recognize as an immediate historical datum. Of course it can examine the lines of development, the growth of traditions, and in that sense can look beyond the individual books to see how they come together to form the one "Scripture." Nevertheless, it always has to begin by going back to the origin of the individual texts, which means placing them in their past context, even if it goes on to complement this move back in time by following up the process through which the texts were later brought together.

We have to keep in mind the limit of all efforts to know the past: We can never go beyond the domain of hypothesis, because we simply cannot bring the past into the present. To be sure, some hypotheses enjoy a high degree of certainty, but overall we need to remain conscious of the limit of our certainties—indeed, the history of modern exegesis makes this limit perfectly evident.

For Reflection

1. What reasons does Pope Benedict XVI give for why the historical-critical method is "an indispensable dimension of exegetical work"?

2. What does the Pope suggest are the limitations of the historical-critical method? Why does he advocate that we should be aware of them?

3. Explain the statement "We can never go beyond the domain of hypothesis, because we simply cannot bring the past into the present." How does the Pope's point relate to the historical-critical method?

Part 4
Overview of the Bible

17 Ignorance of Scripture Is Ignorance of Christ

Introduction

As mentioned in chapter 8, Saint Jerome was the first great Bible scholar in the Latin Western half of the Christian Roman Empire. He produced the first complete Latin translation of the Bible, known as the Vulgate, from the Hebrew and Greek originals of the Old and New Testaments.

Around the time of Jerome, in the fourth and fifth centuries, many Christians neglected to study the Old Testament. Some extreme groups, such as the **Marcionites** and **Gnostics,** even sought to remove the Old Testament from the canon and deny its status as Sacred Scripture. Jerome warned against such a division of interest. Agreeing with other early Christian leaders, Jerome argued that the treasures of salvation found in Christ are established and promised in the Old Testament.

Marcionites A heretical group that promoted the teachings of the second-century heretic Marcion, who rejected the Old Covenant and who wanted to separate Christianity completely from its Jewish roots.

Gnostics From the Greek word *gnosis,* meaning "knowledge." A heretical group that believed Jesus was only a spirit who came to earth to give a select group of people knowledge as the key to salvation.

One must read both the Old and New Testaments to fully understand the saving power of God in Christ, and the two are essential for Scripture study. Jerome's words demand that we not choose one over another; we fully require both to understand God's saving power in Christ. Limiting your knowledge of Scripture in either Testament is limiting your relationship with God.

In this chapter's selection, from *Commentary on Isaiah,* Jerome emphasizes the importance of the Old Testament prophecies contained in the Book of Isaiah and what they reveal about Jesus Christ.

Excerpt from *Commentary on Isaiah*

By Saint Jerome

For if, as Paul says, Christ is the power of God and the wisdom of God, and if the man who does not know Scripture does not know the power and wisdom of God, then ignorance of Scripture is ignorance of Christ.

Therefore, I will imitate the head of a household who brings out of his storehouse things both new and old, and says to his spouse in the Song of Songs: *I have kept for you things new and old, my beloved.* In this way permit me to explain Isaiah, showing that he was not only a prophet, but an evangelist and an apostle as well. For he says about himself and the other evangelists: *How beautiful are the feet of those who preach good news, of those who announce peace.* And God speaks to him as if he were an apostle: *Whom shall I send, who will go to my people?* And he answers: *Here I am; send me.*

No one should think that I mean to explain the entire subject matter of this great book of Scripture in one brief sermon, since it contains all the mysteries of the Lord. It prophesies that Emmanuel ("God with us") is to be born of a virgin and accomplish marvel-

> **Emmanuel**
>
> The name Emmanuel means "God is with us." It first appears with Isaiah's prophecy that a child would soon be born in Jerusalem (see Isaiah 7:14). At that time (ca. 722 BC), Jerusalem was being attacked by the Assyrian army. The child's birth would be a sign that God was present and would defend his people. The Gospel of Matthew cites this verse as being fulfilled in the birth of Christ, who, in the Incarnation, is truly God with us (see Matthew 1:23).

lous works and signs. It predicts his death, burial and resurrection from the dead as the Savior of all men. I need say nothing about the natural sciences, ethics and logic. Whatever is proper to holy Scripture, whatever can be expressed in human language and understood by the human mind, is contained in the book of Isaiah. Of these mysteries the author himself testifies when he writes: *You will be given a vision of all things, like words in a sealed scroll. When they give the writings to a wise man, they will say: Read this. And he will reply: I cannot, for it is sealed. And when the scroll is given to an uneducated man and he is told: Read this, he will reply: I do not know how to read.*

Should this argument appear weak to anyone, let him listen to the Apostle: *Let two or three prophets speak, and let others interpret; if, however, a revelation should come to one of those who are seated there, let the first one be quiet.* How can they be silent, since it depends on the Spirit who speaks through his prophets whether they remain silent or speak? If they understood what they were saying, all things would be full of wisdom and knowledge.

> " *But it was not the air vibrating with the human voice that reached their ears, but rather it was God speaking within the soul of the prophets* "

But it was not the air vibrating with the human voice that reached their ears, but rather it was God speaking within the soul of the prophets, just as another prophet says: *It is an angel who spoke in me;* and again, *Crying out in our hearts, 'Abba, Father',* and I shall listen to what the Lord God says within me.

For Reflection

1.   Jerome says that "ignorance of Scripture is ignorance of Christ." How can study of Old Testament stories and prophecies help us to better understand Christ and the New Testament?

2.   Explain what Jerome means when he says he will imitate the bridegroom from the Song of Songs: "I have kept for you things new and old, my beloved."

3.   Jerome says that Isaiah "was not only a prophet, but an evangelist and an apostle as well." What examples does Jerome give, and how do they reveal Isaiah to have been an evangelist and an apostle?

18 The Relationship between the Church and the Jewish Scriptures

Introduction

In 2002 the Pontifical Biblical Institute published the document *The Jewish People and Their Sacred Scriptures in the Christian Bible*. The Institute sought in part to reaffirm the relationship of the Church to the Jewish people after centuries of tension and, at times, of mistreatment of Jews by Christians. At various times throughout Christian history, the Jews have been accused of deicide, which literally means "murder of God," because some Christians have blamed the Jews for the Crucifixion of Christ. However, the Second Vatican Council's document *Declaration on the Relation of the Church to Non-Christian Religions (Nostra Aetate, 1965)* established a turning point in the strained relationship by praising the Jewish people for their faith, tradition, and stewardship of God's revealed Word in their Sacred Scriptures. *The Jewish People and Their Sacred Scriptures in the Christian Bible* further affirms the relationships between the Church and the Jewish faith by exploring the ways in which the Sacred Scriptures of the two faiths are interconnected.

Although the Church holds that the Old Testament, also known as the Hebrew Scriptures, is fulfilled only in the person of Christ, the Church shows reverence to the texts and the Hebrew tradition that prophesy and offer the foundation and proof of God's salvation in Jesus of Nazareth—who is the new Moses, the Son of David, King of Israel, and Son of God. In respecting the Hebrew Scriptures and the tradition that surrounds them, the Church also embraces the Truth that Judaism has been entrusted with the responsibility of revealing to humanity the teachings of the Law, the Prophets, and the Writings. *The Jewish People and Their Sacred Scriptures in the Christian Bible* emphatically holds to the united tradition and theological purpose of the Hebrew Scriptures and New Testament in revealing God's will to his people.

This document also expresses the relationship between Jewish tradition and the development of Sacred Scripture in a process that parallels the process seen in the early Christian development of the New Testament. Both Testaments were initiated and closed by Tradition. Because of this, Scripture—in its unity—testifies that it alone cannot fully reveal God's inspired Word to its readers and hearers. Rather, the texts must be illumined by the Spirit and read in the light of the apostolic Tradition.

Excerpt from *The Jewish People and Their Sacred Scriptures in the Christian Bible*
By the Pontifical Biblical Commission

Scripture and Oral Tradition in Judaism and Christianity

9. In many religions there exists a tension between Scripture and Tradition. This is true of Oriental Religions (Hinduism, Buddhism, etc.) and Islam. The written texts can never express the Tradition in an exhaustive manner. They have to be completed by additions and interpretations which are eventually written down but are subject to certain limitations. This phenomenon can be seen in Christianity as well as in Judaism, with developments that are partly similar and partly different. A common trait is that both share a significant part of the same canon of Scripture.

1. Scripture and Tradition in the Old Testament and Judaism

Tradition gives birth to Scripture. The origin of Old Testament texts and the history of the formation of the canon have been the subject of important works in the last few years. A certain consensus has been reached according to which by the end of the first century of our era, the long process of the formation of the Hebrew Bible was practically completed. This canon comprised the *Tŏr~h,* the Prophets and the greater part of the "Writings." To determine the origin of the individual books is often a difficult task. In many cases, one must settle for hypotheses. These are, for the most part, based on results furnished by Form, Tradition and Redaction Criticism. It can be deduced from them that ancient precepts were assembled in collections which were gradually inserted in the books of the Pentateuch. The older narratives were likewise committed to writing and arranged together. Collections of narrative texts and rules of conduct were combined. Prophetic messages were collected and compiled in books bearing the prophets' names. The **sapiential texts,** Psalms and didactic narratives were likewise collected much later.

Over time Tradition produced a "second Scripture" **(Mishna).** No written text can adequately express all the riches of a tradition. The biblical sacred texts left open many questions concerning the proper understanding of Israelite faith and conduct. That gave rise, in Pharisaic and Rabbinic Judaism, to a long process of written texts, from the

"Mishna" ("Second Text"), edited at the beginning of the third century by Jehuda ha-Nasi, to the "Tosepta" ("Supplement") and **Talmud** in its two-fold form (Babylonian and Jerusalem). Notwithstanding its authority, this interpretation by itself was not deemed adequate in later times, with the result that later rabbinic explanations were added. These additions were never granted the same authority as the Talmud, they served only as an aid to interpretation. Unresolved questions were submitted to the decisions of the Grand Rabbinate.

In this manner, written texts gave rise to further developments. Between written texts and oral tradition a certain sustained tension is evident.

The Limits of Tradition. When it was put into writing to be joined to Scripture, a normative Tradition, for all that, never enjoyed the same authority as Scripture. It did not become part of the "Writings which soil the hands", that is, "which are sacred" and was not accepted as such in the liturgy. The Mishna, the Tosepta and the Talmud have their place in the synagogue as texts to be studied, but they are not read in the liturgy. Generally, a tradition is evaluated by its conformity to the *Tôr-h.* The reading of the *Tôr-h* occupies a privileged place in the liturgy of the Synagogue. To it are added pericopes chosen from the Prophets. According to

Tôr-h (Torah) This term means different things in different situations. Generally, it is the revelation of God's will to the people; more specifically, it is the divine Law, especially as contained in the first five books of the Bible, which together are commonly called the Torah.

sapiential texts The wisdom books or writings found in the Old Testament, including Proverbs, Ecclesiastes, Song of Songs, Wisdom, and Sirach.

Mishna Written down about AD 200, the Mishna (often spelled Mishnah) contains collected teachings of the rabbis of the preceding four centuries. Along with the Talmud, it is the most important text of the oral narratives of the revelation of God's will, or Torah.

Talmud The vast depository of the oral Torah, based on the Mishnah with extensive rabbinic commentary on each chapter. There are two versions, the Jerusalem (completed about AD 300) and the Babylonian (completed about 450).

ancient Jewish belief, the *Tōr‑h* was conceived before the creation of the world. The Samaritans accept only the *Tōr‑h* as Sacred Scripture, while the Sadducees reject every normative Tradition outside the Law and the Prophets. Conversely, Pharisaic and Rabbinic Judaism accept, alongside the written Law, an oral Law given simultaneously to Moses and enjoying the same authority. A tract in the Mishna states: "At Sinai, Moses received the oral Law and handed it on to Joshua, and Joshua to the ancestors, and the ancestors to the prophets, and the prophets handed it on to members of the Great Synagogue" (Aboth 1:1). Clearly, a striking diversity is apparent from the manner of conceiving the role of Tradition.

Scripture and Tradition in Early Christianity

10. *Tradition gives birth to Scripture.* In early Christianity, an evolution similar to that of Judaism can be observed with, however, an initial difference: early Christians had the Scriptures from the very beginning, since as Jews, they accepted Israel's Bible as Scripture. But for them an oral tradition was added on, "the teaching of the Apostles" (Ac 2:42), which handed on the words of Jesus and the narrative of events concerning him. The Gospel catechesis took shape only gradually. To better ensure their faithful transmission, the words of Jesus and the narratives were put in writing. Thus, the way was prepared for the redaction of the Gospels which took place some decades after the death and resurrection of Jesus. In addition, professions of faith were also composed, together with the liturgical hymns

> 66 *Christianity has in common with Judaism the conviction that God's revelation cannot be expressed in its entirety in written texts.* 99

which are found in the New Testament Letters. The Letters of Paul and the other apostles or leaders were first read in the church for which they were written (cf. 1 Th 5:27), were passed on to other churches (cf. Col 4:16), preserved to be read on other occasions and eventually accepted as Scripture (cf. 2 P 3:15–16) and attached to the Gospels. In this way, the canon of the New Testament was gradually formed within the apostolic Tradition.

Tradition completes Scripture. Christianity has in common with Judaism the conviction that God's revelation cannot be expressed in its entirety in written texts. This is clear from the ending of the Fourth Gospel where it is stated that the whole world would be unable to contain the books that could be written recounting the actions of Jesus (Jn 21:25). On the other hand, a vibrant tradition is indispensable to make Scripture come alive and maintain its relevance.

It is worth recalling here the teaching of the **Farewell Discourse** on the role of "the Spirit of truth" after Jesus' departure. He will remind the disciples of all that Jesus said (Jn 14:26), bear witness on Jesus' behalf (15:26), and lead the disciples "into all the truth" (16:13), giving them a deeper understanding of the person of Christ, his message and work. As a result of the Spirit's action, the tradition remains alive and dynamic.

Having affirmed that the apostolic preaching is found "expressed in a special way" (*"speciali modo exprimitur"*) in the inspired Books, the Second Vatican Council observes that it is Tradition "that renders a more profound understanding in the Church of Sacred Scripture and makes it always effective" (*Dei Verbum* 8). Scripture is defined as the "Word of God committed to writing under the inspiration of the Holy Spirit"; but it is Tradition that "transmits to the successors of the apostles the Word of God entrusted by Christ the Lord and by the Holy Spirit to the apostles, so that, illumined by the Spirit of truth, they will protect it faithfully, explain it and make it known by their preaching" (*DV* 9). The Council concludes: "Consequently, it is not from Sacred Scripture alone that the Church draws its certainty about everything which has been revealed" and adds: "That is why both—Scripture and Tradition—must be accepted and venerated with the same sense of devotion and reverence" (*DV* 9).

The Limits of the additional contribution of Tradition. To what extent can there be in the Christian Church a tradition that is a material addition to the word of Scripture? This question has long been debated in the history of theology. The Second

farewell discourse A form of literature in which a person who is soon to die says farewell to his friends, often by leaving instructions. The Gospel of John presents Jesus' Farewell Discourse to his disciples in chapters 14–17.

Vatican Council appears to have left the matter open, but at least declined to speak of "two sources of revelation," which would be Scripture and Tradition; it affirmed instead that "Sacred Tradition and Sacred Scripture constitute a unique sacred deposit of the Word of God which is entrusted to the Church" (*Dei Verbum* 10). It likewise rejected the idea of a tradition completely independent of Scripture. On one point at least, the Council mentions an additional contribution made by Tradition, one of great importance: Tradition "enabled the Church to recognise the full canon of the Sacred Books" (*DV* 8). Here, the extent to which Scripture and Tradition are inseparable can be seen.

For Reflection

1. According to the reading, what are the differences between the Torah and the Mishna? Why is the Torah read in the Jewish liturgy, while the Mishna is not?

2. For the Catholic Church how does Tradition complete the Scriptures?

3. Explain the parallels between the development of Scripture and Tradition in the Jewish faith and in early Christianity.

19 Unity of the Old and New Testaments

Introduction

In the previous two chapters, we read how the Old Testament serves as the foundation for what is found in the New Testament. The reading from Saint Jerome focused on the importance of studying the Old Testament to find knowledge of Christ that will enhance one's relationship with God. The reading from the Pontifical Biblical Commission established the historical and traditional connections between the Hebrew canon and the Greek New Testament. This chapter now focuses on the theological interrelatedness of the two Testaments. The Old and New Testaments require each other. Each tells only one part of an important story: God's plan to save and renew humanity and all of creation.

As mentioned in previous chapters, the Church has faced opposition from groups who wished to discount or ignore the Old Testament. As this chapter's reading demonstrates, however, the Church has always taught that the Old Testament is "indispensable" as Scripture, because the original covenant with Israel has never been revoked. The Word of God is active and effective in both Testaments. The Old Testament points forward to God's fulfillment of the Scriptures in Jesus Christ and to the presence of the Spirit in the Church. Both still await complete fulfillment in God's judgment of creation and renewal of creation (see Daniel, chapters 7–12; Romans, chapters 5–8).

The reading for this chapter comes from the universal *Catechism,* or the *Catechism of the Catholic Church (CCC)*. The excerpt is from the section that defines the meaning and limits of the canon of Scripture. Its purpose is to respond to those who have tried to diminish or even refute the Old Testament's stature in the canon. The Church depends on the sacred texts that foretell the arrival of the Savior and the hope that all humanity will find justice and renewal with God.

Excerpt from the *Catechism of the Catholic Church*

The Old Testament

The Old Testament is an indispensable part of Sacred Scripture. Its books are divinely inspired and retain a permanent value,[1] for the Old Covenant has never been revoked.

Indeed, "the economy of the Old Testament was deliberately so oriented that it should prepare for and declare in prophecy the coming of Christ, redeemer of all men."[2] "Even though they contain matters imperfect and provisional,"[3] the books of the Old Testament bear witness to the whole divine **pedagogy** of God's saving love: these writings "are a storehouse of sublime teaching on God and of sound wisdom on human life, as well as a wonderful treasury of prayers; in them, too, the mystery of our salvation is present in a hidden way."[4]

> *Christians venerate the Old Testament as true Word of God.*

Christians venerate the Old Testament as true Word of God. The Church has always vigorously opposed the idea of rejecting the Old Testament under the pretext that the New has rendered it void (Marcionism).

The New Testament

"The Word of God, which is the power of God for salvation to everyone who has faith, is set forth and displays its power in a most wonderful way in the writings of the New Testa-

pedagogy A method or strategy used in teaching.

ment[5] which hand on the ultimate truth of God's Revelation. Their central object is Jesus Christ, God's incarnate Son: his acts, teachings, Passion and glorification, and his Church's beginnings under the Spirit's guidance."[6]

The *Gospels* are the heart of all the Scriptures "because they are our principal source for the life and teaching of the Incarnate Word, our Saviour."[7]

Endnotes

1. Cf. *Dei Verbum* 14.
2. *Dei Verbum* 15.
3. *Dei Verbum* 15.
4. *Dei Verbum* 15.
5. *Dei Verbum*17; cf. *Romans* 1:16.
6. Cf. *Dei Verbum* 20.
7. *Dei Verbum*18.

For Reflection

1. What reasons does this reading give to explain why "the Old Testament is an indispensable part of Sacred Scripture"?

2. Why are "the Gospels the heart of all the Scriptures"?

3. Based on this reading and previous readings in this text, explain the relationship between the Old and New Testaments.

20 The Council of Trent: Closing the Canon of Authoritative Scripture

Introduction

The Council of Trent (1545–1563), the Church's sixteenth Ecumenical Council, was convened in response to the Protestant Reformation. The Council bishops convened several sessions over an extended period of time to discuss a number of the topics the reformers had broached, including the selling of indulgences, the structure and content of the *Catechism,* and many aspects of the liturgy.

The fourth session of the Council was devoted to the Scriptures. This session established the proper canon, or list of books considered to be authoritative, sacred, and revelatory for the faith and morals of the faithful. This decree was necessary for several reasons. First, some Protestant reformers had changed the list of books that were in the Bible. Many eliminated books of the Old Testament, such as Tobit, Judith, Sirach (Ecclesiasticus), and Wisdom. Martin Luther relegated the Book of Revelation to an appendix in his German New Testament and threatened to remove the Epistle of James altogether (though he later retained it). A second development that made the decree necessary was the invention of the printing press in the mid-fifteenth century, which made it possible for printers to publish bibles that were not authorized translations. Some of these published bibles left books out or included incorrect translations or notes without explaining the identity of the author or publisher. The Council's decree clarified authoritatively the books to be considered sacred. Finally, the decree closed the discussion of the canon that had begun as early as the Council of Nicaea in 325. The matters of the canon had been discussed at Nicaea and were affirmed at the Council of Hippo in 419, but they were not definitively closed. The problems that arose from the Reformation demonstrated that the discussions of the earlier Councils required decisive closure to eliminate future problems.

The decree is still essential for us today, particularly because it teaches about the importance of, and the process behind, our canon of Scripture. The canon was set through a process of discussion and discernment. Bishops in Councils across empires and centuries had discussed, discerned, and prayed about which books should be considered sacred and useful for the instruction of the faithful. This decree represents the final product of this process.

Excerpt from *Decree Concerning the Canonical Scriptures*
By the Council of Trent

The sacred and holy, ecumenical, and general Synod of Trent,—lawfully assembled in the Holy Ghost, the same three legates of the Apostolic See presiding therein,—keeping this always in view, that, errors being removed, the purity itself of the Gospel be preserved in the Church; which (Gospel), before promised through the prophets in the holy Scriptures, our Lord Jesus Christ, the Son of God, first promulgated with His

The Protestant Reformation

The Protestant Reformation began with Martin Luther's Ninety-Five Theses, written in 1517. Luther questioned the selling of indulgences and the requirement of celibacy for clergy, and he wanted the Bible and Mass translated into German and other local languages. He refused to retract all of his writings at the demand of Pope Leo X in 1520 and the Holy Roman Emperor Charles V, and consequently the Pope excommunicated him, and the emperor condemned him as an outlaw. Followers of Martin Luther became known as Lutherans. His teachings are the basis of many Protestant beliefs and practices today.

> 66 *(The Synod,) following the examples of the orthodox Fathers, receives and venerates with an equal affection of piety, and reverence, all the books both of the Old and of the New Testament—seeing that one God is the author of both.* 99

own mouth, and then commanded to be preached by His Apostles to every creature, as the fountain of all, both saving truth, and moral discipline; and seeing clearly that this truth and discipline are contained in the written books, and the unwritten traditions which, received by the Apostles from the mouth of Christ himself, or from the Apostles themselves, the Holy Ghost dictating, have come down even unto us, transmitted as it were from hand to hand; (the Synod) following the examples of the **orthodox Fathers,** receives and venerates with an equal affection of piety, and reverence, all the books both of the Old and of the New Testament—seeing that one God is the author of both—as also the said traditions, as well those appertaining to faith as to morals, as having been dictated, either by Christ's own word of mouth, or by the Holy Ghost, and preserved in the Catholic Church by a continuous succession. And it has thought it meet that a list of the sacred books be inserted in this decree, lest a doubt may arise in any one's mind, which are the books that are received by this Synod. They are as set down here below: of the Old Testament: the five books of Moses, to wit, Genesis, Exodus, Leviticus, Numbers, Deuteronomy; Josue, Judges, Ruth, **four books of Kings,** two of **Paralipomenon,** the first book of Esdras, and the second which is entitled Nehemias; Tobias, Judith, Esther, Job, the Davidical Psalter, consisting of a hundred and fifty psalms; the Proverbs,

orthodox Fathers Early theologians and leaders who had the "correct teaching" (the literal meaning of *orthodox*) regarding the books of Scripture. Taken broadly, this would include leaders such as Ignatius of Antioch (ca. 50–105?) and Justin Martyr (ca. 115–200), up to the Council Fathers of Nicaea and Hippo.

four books of Kings In the Greek Old Testament, 1 and 2 Samuel and 1 and 2 Kings were named 1, 2, 3, and 4 Kings.

Paralipomenon The Greek name for the books of Chronicles.

anathema A ban declared by the Church that involves excommunication.

Ecclesiastes, the Canticle of Canticles, Wisdom, Ecclesiasticus, Isaias, Jeremias, with Baruch; Ezechiel, Daniel; the twelve minor prophets, to wit, Osee, Joel, Amos, Abdias, Jonas, Micheas, Nahum, Habacuc, Sophonias, Aggæus, Zacharias, Malachias; two books of the Machabees, the first and the second. Of the New Testament: the four Gospels, according to Matthew, Mark, Luke, and John; the Acts of the Apostles written by Luke the Evangelist; fourteen epistles of Paul the apostle, (one) to the Romans, two to the Corinthians, (one) to the Galatians, to the Ephesians, to the Philippians, to the Colossians, two to the Thessalonians, two to Timothy, (one) to Titus, to Philemon, to the Hebrews; two of Peter the apostle, three of John the apostle, one of the apostle James, one of Jude the apostle, and the Apocalypse of John the apostle. But if any one receive not, as sacred and canonical, the said books entire with all their parts, as they have been used to be read in the Catholic Church, and as they are contained in the old Latin vulgate edition; and knowingly and deliberately contemn the traditions aforesaid; let him be **anathema.** Let all, therefore, understand, in what order, and in what manner, the said Synod, after having laid the foundation of the Confession of faith, will proceed, and what testimonies and authorities it will mainly use in confirming dogmas, and in restoring morals in the Church.

For Reflection

1. How does this reading explain the role of Tradition in setting the canon of Scripture?

2. According to the reading, what criteria did the Council of Trent use for determining which books it would receive into the canon of Scripture?

3. In the conclusion of this reading, what are the stated results of the setting of the canon of Scripture?

21 The Formation of Scripture: Traditions, Texts, and Canons

Introduction

Because we often engage with the Bible as a single text, believers can at times treat it as if it appeared suddenly one day in its finished form. The Bible does not represent a single authorial tradition. Rather, it is the culmination of years of oral tradition and historical experiences. In this chapter's reading, the scholar Marielle Frigge, OSB, explains the four-step process of how the Bible has developed from ancient examples of cultural memory into an authoritative collection of books. This chapter's selection, from her work *Beginning Biblical Studies,* serves to outline the major developments in the origins of the Old and New Testaments.

Both canons, the Old and New Testaments, began with events in the life of the faithful that were then told and retold in an expanding body of oral traditions. Often these events were shared and passed on in different communities, thereby leading to different oral traditions of the same events. These different traditions began to develop their own particular emphases in the telling of the stories. For example, one tradition in the Torah tells the stories of Israel's origins by focusing on the characters' human failings and the need for God's mercy and salvation (Genesis, chapters 2–3, 15). Another tradition that covers many of the same stories emphasizes how humanity is able to understand and do God's will because we are made in his divine image (Genesis, chapters 1, 17). Both traditions fill out the larger picture of Israel's origins by pointing to particular aspects of a theological truth.

These oral traditions are often symbolic rather than fixed, and therefore they more effectively explain a theological truth than provide a factual history lesson. For example, the story of Genesis, chapter 27, is full of extraordinary events involving Isaac and his sons, Esau and Jacob. No matter how these events really took place, the point of the story is that God worked through the reality of people's many limitations to bring his covenant to Israel, the descendants of Jacob.

Eventually these oral traditions were written down. An example of this is the Torah, which appears to be made up of four or more different oral traditions. The final step in the process of the formation of the Bible was the establishment of an authoritative list of the books that had been written down. These lists were decided by bodies of religious leaders who followed a set of criteria. Rabbinic leaders formed the Hebrew Bible canon in AD 90, and the bishops at the Council of Nicaea outlined the New Testament canon in AD 325, which was later set at the Council of Trent (1545–1563). In both cases Tradition shaped the canon by influencing both the criteria by which the books were judged and the group of leaders who served in selecting these books. Guided by the Holy Spirit, each stage of this process—from events to oral traditions to written traditions to the setting of the canon—has resulted in the sacred text we know as the Bible.

Excerpt from *Beginning Biblical Studies*

By Marielle Frigge

Formation of the Bible: A Four-Stage Process

1. EVENTS: A People's History Interpreted as Experiences of the Divine

Before proceeding it is important to point out that the books in the Bible were not written in the order in which they now appear. The most formative experience—and one of the earliest formed traditions—in Old Testament history, the Exodus, is not found at the very beginning of the Bible. This event of Exodus, the liberation of Hebrew slaves from Egypt, was understood to reveal Yahweh as Israel's mighty deliverer and to designate the Hebrews as a people, a community belonging to Yahweh. This foundational saving event began a centuries-long history of the relationship between the God of Israel and Yahweh's chosen people. Further experiences in Israelite history were interpreted as ongoing revelation of God and God's life-giving plan for all creation. Eventually, stories about the origin of the world and of Israel were also preserved and placed at the beginning of the sacred writings.

2. ORAL TRADITIONS: Events and Their Religious Meanings Passed On by Word of Mouth

Israel's experiences of Yahweh, and most importantly, the religious significance of those experiences, were considered so important that the faith community passed them on from generation to generation in oral traditions. A primarily oral culture, ancient Israel employed numerous spoken forms

> " *Cultures that normally transmit important material by word of mouth are highly accurate in communicating essential material.* "

such as legends, poetry, prayers, law codes, and **genealogies** to tell the story of their relationship with Yahweh. Modern readers, however, are cautioned against imagining the process of oral tradition like a game of "telephone" in which every successive repetition loses or distorts the original meaning. Cultures that normally transmit important material by word of mouth are highly accurate in communicating essential material. Because important events and ideas are passed on by and within a highly attentive community accustomed to such communication, any mistakes are quickly identified and easily corrected.

Thus while orally transmitted material may vary in details, it preserves accuracy in essential meaning. This quality of oral tradition can be seen today in jokes told and retold in various contexts; those who pass on the joke might change geographical details

genealogy A type of family tree, or a bloodline. A genealogy is also a literary genre used as a proclamation to make connections with important ancestors.

to suit their own locale, but the all-important punch-line remains essentially the same. A second earmark of oral tradition is that it is not overly concerned with factual accuracy about when, where, and how events happened; it is the significance of such happenings that is emphasized. Today, a man telling his children about how he met their mother might at one time say they shared lunch and another time describe a wonderful dinner; what will remain unchanged, however, will be the fact that he was immediately attracted by her charming sense of humor. Third, in order to highlight the significance of certain experiences, oral tradition often describes people and events as bigger than life. A modern example would be the well-known "fish story": perhaps a small child struggles for five minutes to land a six-inch fish, but retold by a proud grandfather who wants to underscore the child's perseverance, the story might describe a two-foot fish that fought for an hour before finally being hauled ashore. Fourth, oral transmission rarely if ever expresses meaning by using precise definitions. Religious interpretations arise out of the experience of the faith community over generations, and such profound significance is communicated best by vivid stories about meaningful events. If someone wishes to understand friendship, for example, a dictionary definition would communicate much less of that reality than a few stories about loyal, faithful friends.

3. WRITTEN TRADITIONS: Selected Material Gathered and Edited into Written Collections

All four earmarks of oral tradition described above are still found in many parts of the Bible, because these characteristics frequently found their way into written traditions. As the Israelites' history stretched across centuries, it became more and more important to preserve accounts of their experience as Yahweh's people. For various reasons, over many years the Israelites were scattered into various parts of the ancient world, and so written traditions were gathered together in diverse historical, geographical, political, and social situations. While written traditions were forming, oral transmission continued as well; as a result, those who compiled written traditions selected and edited writings based on a broad range of sources, always keeping in mind the perspective and needs of the particular group for whom the material was composed. Sometimes writers presented the same essential content in variant accounts derived from different sources without bothering to explain or reconcile inconsistencies. For example, at one point in the story of Noah, God instructs Noah to take one pair of every kind of animal into the ark; however, a few verses later God requires seven pairs of some animals and one pair of others (Gen 6:19–20, 7:2–3). Such seeming contradictions indicate the use of several written sources in composing a single book.

4. CANONS ESTABLISHED: Authoritative Writings Determined by Faith Community

The word *canon* comes from Greek *kanon,* meaning a rule or measure; the term thus implies both criteria used to measure something and the result of such testing. In general, a canon refers to a collection of works considered authoritative because they have met a particular standard or measure.

New Testament Criteria

Four standards, or criteria, were used to discern the validity of a book as being divinely inspired when the canon of the New Testament was established. First, a book had to be written by an Apostle or his disciple to demonstrate a close connection to Jesus. Second, the book had to be universally accepted by all major Christian communities of the early Church. Third, the books had to be used widely by the early Church in liturgy, most importantly when the early Christians gathered for the Eucharist. Finally, the message of the book had to be consistent with other Christian and Jewish writings.

For example, professional musicians speak of the canon of Western music, and literary experts refer to the canon of American literature. In relation to the Bible, the canon is the set of writings accepted as having supreme authority for faith life; writings designated as canonical have measured up to certain criteria, and so are included in the Bible. It is important to realize that canonization of certain Scriptures resulted from a lengthy communal process rather than the decision of a single religious leader or council. Writings that were repeatedly and consistently used for prayer, guidance, teaching, and interpretation of the community's experience with God gradually gained acceptance as normative for the community's faith, thus becoming canonical. However, as already noted, there are several different canons and so several different Bibles.

For Reflection

1. In your own words summarize the four stages in the process of the formation of the Bible.

2. Explain the four "earmarks" of oral tradition as presented in this reading.

3. According to the reading, why was it necessary for the Israelites to move from oral tradition to written tradition? How did the presence of different oral traditions affect the written tradition?

4. The reading explains that the same story is sometimes told in two or more different ways in the Scriptures. Compare Genesis, chapters 15 and 17. Both are from oral traditions of God's covenant with Abraham. What theological truth does each point to? What symbols are explained in each? What basic truth do both agree on?

Part 5
The Gospels

22 A Glorious Puzzle: The Formation of the Gospels

Introduction

The story behind the development of the Gospels presents us with an incredible puzzle. From the early days of the Church, scholars have considered how the Gospels arrived at their present forms. This debate has been dominated by three different ways of thinking, with the third now being considered the most likely.

In the first hypothesis, scholars thought of the Gospel authors as individuals who were giving their own accounts. Just as different people who witness the same car accident may provide slightly different accounts, similarities and variations may have developed in the Gospel writers' accounts. As a result, some first thought that Matthew and John wrote their own accounts, Mark wrote down Peter's account, and Luke gathered his account from other eyewitnesses.

Other scholars preferred a second hypothesis that considered the similarities and differences to have come from various oral traditions. Stories about Jesus were told and retold in various narrative lines, and at some point these were collected by different authors. This theory is sometimes called the "pearl" theory, because it suggests that the authors gathered together the oral narratives about Jesus as one places pearls on a string to make a necklace.

In more recent scholarship, however, a third idea has become more prominent: the Gospel authors are similar because they have a literary relationship, meaning that some of them used

"Q" A hypothetical source of sayings, used by the authors of Matthew and Luke.

one another's works as sources. In the reading below, Christopher McMahon, PhD, describes the formation of the Gospels and then presents the two-source hypothesis, which holds that Mark wrote first (around AD 70). Then, not knowing each other, Matthew and Luke both wrote in the 80s using Mark's text and another hypothetical source of sayings, simply called "**Q.**" Meanwhile, some scholars now believe that the Gospel of John developed independently of the other three Gospels.

The understanding of the formation of the Gospels that is presented in this reading aids the modern reader in mapping out the origins and relationships of the Gospels to one another. Additionally, the reading provides helpful information for studying each Gospel in comparison to its sources. All of this benefits the reader's understanding of each Gospel, bringing the reader closer to studying the words of Christ at a deeper level.

Excerpt from *Saint Mary's Press® College Study Bible: Introduction to the Gospels and the Acts of the Apostles*

By Christopher McMahon

The Formation of the Gospel Accounts

Since the early twentieth century, biblical scholars have wrestled with how the Gospel tradition was formed. In 1964, the Pontifical Biblical Commission, then a teaching office of the Vatican, outlined the Roman Catholic Church's understanding of the development of the material

> **❝ The Gospels developed in three distinct yet interdependent stages. ❞**

in the Gospels (*Sancta Mater Ecclesia*). This account, reaffirmed at Vatican Council II in the *Dogmatic Constitution on Divine Revelation* (*Dei Verbum,* no. 19), states that the Gospels developed in three distinct yet interdependent stages. What follows is a summary of how New Testament scholarship generally views these three stages.

Stage I: The early followers of Jesus witness his proclamation of the nearness of God's Kingdom by word (pronouncements and parables) and action (symbolic actions and miraculous signs). Jesus' own role in the coming Kingdom is central. Jesus challenges the contemporary boundaries of Judaism, including prohibitions against table fellowship with known sinners and outcasts. He also calls into question the function of the Temple and confronts the religious and political establishment.

Stage II: The early followers of Jesus, almost all of whom had abandoned him at his hour of need, now proclaim him "Lord" and "Savior" in light of their experience of his Resurrection from the dead and the outpouring of the Spirit. Saul of Tarsus is converted to become a follower of Christ and embarks on a missionary career, leaving behind letters that he had written to various churches giving instructions on a wide variety of issues. Much of the apostolic preaching, or *kērygma,* contains little information about Jesus' life and ministry, though many remembrances of his pronouncements, miracles, and controversies are preserved in a variety of contexts by the early Christian church.

Stage III: The proclamation of Jesus' saving work begins to take on a more narrative structure and gives way to the formation of the written Gospel accounts. These narratives incorporate material from both of the previous stages; however, they build a distinct portrait of Christ for the contemporary Christian Church.

These three stages illustrate the movement of the Gospel from the Apostles' experience of Jesus to an oral proclamation of the Good News, and then to a literary proclamation as well. This process or movement was accompanied by the development of a theology that sought to integrate more closely the life of Jesus with the proclamation of his Resurrection.

kērygma A Greek word meaning "proclamation" or "preaching," referring to the announcement of the Gospel or the Good News of divine salvation offered to all through Jesus Christ. The word has two senses. It is both an event of proclamation and a message proclaimed.

Upon reading the first three canonical narratives about Jesus, commonly called the synoptic Gospels, the reader is struck by both the great number of verbal and structural similarities and by the uniqueness of many of the stories (the word *synoptic* means "seen together"). The precise nature and extent of the literary relationships among these texts has been an issue for centuries and is called "the synoptic problem." In the nineteenth century the long-accepted priority of Matthew fell under suspicion, and Scripture scholars like K. Lachmann began to argue for the priority of Mark over Matthew and Luke. These scholars believed that Matthew and Luke started with the Gospel of Mark, which Matthew and Luke revised and to which they added material. This theory helped to explain the material common to all three synoptic accounts, yet there remained

> ### Four Gospels, One Truth
>
> In the Bible we find four unique Gospels sharing the life, Passion, death, and Resurrection of Jesus Christ. Together all four Gospels help us to understand God's love and saving actions in Jesus Christ, his Incarnate Son. Though the Gospels recount similar stories and experiences, each one presents a unique portrait of Jesus. Even though the Gospels may differ in some details, they will never contradict one another on the essential truths of the mystery of Christ, including his Incarnation, life, Passion, death, Resurrection, and Ascension.

the problem of the two-hundred-twenty verses shared only by Luke and Matthew. In an effort to account for these verses, C. Weisse erected the so-called two-source hypothesis. He posited the existence of a collection of sayings from Jesus that circulated in the early church, and this source was eventually designated by the letter Q, an abbreviation for the German word *Quelle,* which means "source." According to the two-source hypothesis, Matthew and Luke had access to Q as well as Mark, when they composed their Gospels. While some scholars are skeptical about the existence of Q, the two-source hypothesis is generally the preferred solution to the synoptic problem.

The Q source is not the only hypothetical source posited by New Testament scholars. There is much material in the New Testament, the origins of which are difficult to determine. The fourth Gospel (John) stands apart from the synoptic Gospels as part of an early and unique tradition of Jesus' life and ministry, even though there are still some important points of contact with the synoptics (e.g., the cleansing of the Temple, walking on the sea, Jesus' entry into Jerusalem). This uniqueness has caused some to consider the material in John to be far removed from the life and ministry of Jesus, yet others (e.g., John Meier) have argued that some of the unique material in John may indeed go back to stage I. But virtually all scholars agree that the vast majority of the material in the Gospel of John reflects the unique theology and concerns of the late first-century Christian church. In addition to the fourth Gospel, scholars struggle to account for special material in Matthew and Luke that is not related to Mark or Q (this material is often designated with the letters **M** and **L**). Like the Johannine material, the special Matthean and Lucan material reflects each of these authors' theological tendencies.

"M" A hypothetical source, used by the author of Matthew's Gospel, that contained stories and sayings of Jesus.

"L" A hypothetical source of stories and sayings of Jesus, used by the author of Luke's Gospel.

For Reflection

1. Identify and explain the three stages of the formation of the Gospels.

2. Summarize the two-source theory as it is presented in this reading. How does it account for the similarities and differences among the three synoptic Gospels?

3. Compare Matthew 14:22–33 with Mark 6:45–52. What is similar, and what is different? How does this comparison reflect the two-source theory? What does Matthew emphasize in the account that is not found in Mark?

23 The Gospel of Matthew

Introduction

In the early Church, Matthew was the most popular and most-cited Gospel. Believed to have been composed between AD 80 and 90, Matthew's Gospel was once thought to be the first Gospel written. For this reason—and because the Gospel's beginning, through the genealogy, connects the life and teachings of Jesus to the writings of the Old Testament—Matthew's Gospel was placed as the opening book of the New Testament. As we saw in earlier chapters, knowing the cultural context of the author and audience is helpful to better understand a text. For the Gospel of Matthew, it is important to recognize the tension between Jewish and Gentile Christians that surrounded the beginning of the Church.

In the decades following the Resurrection, the early Church was immersed in Jewish heritage and culture. Jesus, his Apostles, and indeed most of the disciples in Jerusalem were Jewish. Jesus was the long-awaited Messiah, the King of Israel, who had arrived and would return again in fulfillment of the Jewish Scriptures. The relationship with God that he embodied in his ministry gave a renewed interpretation of God's covenant with Israel in the Law.

But tensions were arising in the early Church. Not all of Israel accepted Jesus as the Messiah, and some non-Jews (**Gentiles**) were beginning to accept and believe in Jesus, his Resurrection, and his return (see Acts, chapters 10–11). Their faith and Baptism joined Gentiles to the community spiritually, but cultural barriers remained. Religious customs were

> **Gentiles** A term used by Jews to describe non-Jews.

in tension with theological reality. How could non-Jews join a covenant and community that appeared to be intended for Israel alone?

This appears to have been a central issue for the community in Antioch, from which the Gospel of Matthew developed. Matthew's Gospel presents Jesus as the fulfillment of the Old Testament and Jewish traditions and, at the same time, also makes room for Gentiles to take part in this faith community without converting to Judaism.

The following reading exploring the Gospel of Matthew comes from Rudolf Schnackenburg, a prominent German Catholic biblical scholar. In this reading Schnackenburg explains major points regarding the authorship, community, composition, and theology of the Gospel of Matthew. The reading is important today because it provides information about the Gospel's background to aid the modern reader's understanding of this rich and powerful presentation of Christ's life and teachings.

Excerpt from *The Gospel of Matthew*
By Rudolf Schnackenburg

1. Form and Construction

The Gospel of Matthew stands at the beginning of the New Testament canon and occupies a primary place in it. It is not, however, the first work of the Gospel genre to appear. The first was the Gospel of Mark, which the author of Matthew knew and used. Why and to what end, then, has "Matthew" (the name will stand for the author, without prejudice to his actual identity) written this great Gospel? That will obviously have connections with the community to which he belongs and for which he writes. . . . He will seek not only to offer this community new material, but also to address it in its situation and to indicate to it what he sees to be the proper direction for a life in accordance with Jesus' message. Although he adopts the geographical framework of the Gospel of Mark and follows much of the arrangement of material used by his predecessor, Matthew has nevertheless created a new work, one that stands on its own.

When we compare Matthew's Gospel with that of Mark, the first elements that strike us are the expansions at the beginning and at the end. Matthew begins with a "prehistory," an account of certain events before the appearance of John the Baptist and before Jesus' baptism. This account, in contrast to the Lukan "infancy narrative," can be called a "Pre-Gospel." First comes a genealogy that focuses on Jesus' descent from David, and before David from Abraham (1:1–17). Next, in an extended appendix to 1:16, the virgin conception of Jesus by the Holy Spirit is announced to Joseph in a revelation (1:18–25). Chapter 2 is intended to establish not only Jesus' birth in Bethlehem, the city of David, and his domicile in Nazareth, but also the destiny of the messianic child as typologically prefigured in the history of Moses. The first two chapters, then, are intended to direct the reader's attention to the person of Jesus Christ from a viewpoint of faith (**christologically**), and to lay the groundwork for the presentation of Jesus' emergence and activity.

At the end of his Gospel, Matthew offers burial and Easter recitals not to be found in Mark, and intended to strengthen faith in Jesus' resurrection (the guarding of the tomb, 27:62–66; 28:11–15; the appearance to the women, 28:9–10), climaxing in Jesus' appearance to the disciples with the commission to go forth to all peoples (28:16–20). These key sections at the beginning and end flank the rest of the Gospel, which develops Jesus' earthly activity of proclamation and teaching, his salvific deeds and struggles against opposition, and finally presents his destiny of passion and death.

But how has the evangelist ordered his material? His structure is the object of widely varying assessments. We can solve the problem, however, by recognizing the turning point at 16:21, after the scene at Caesarea Philippi. In 4:17 we read, "From that time Jesus began to proclaim . . . ," and in 16:21 we read the formally similar "From that time on, Jesus began to show his disciples that he must go to Jerusalem and undergo much suffering." After the introduction (the emergence of John the Baptist, Jesus'

> **christological** Related to Christology, the branch of theology that studies the person and life of Jesus Christ, his ministry, and his mission.

> ### The Author of Matthew's Gospel
>
> The Gospel of Matthew was once thought to be written by the Apostle Matthew. It is now believed, however, that the Gospel was written by an unknown Jewish Christian, most likely in Antioch, the capital of Syria. The author was writing for a mixed community of Jewish Christians and Gentiles and sought to communicate to them that salvation was possible without conversion to the Jewish faith.

baptism and temptation, and the beginning of his work in Galilee, 3:1—4:16), the first part covers Jesus' public proclamation and activity in Galilee, but with great effect in a wider area (cf. 4:24–25). The second part recounts Jesus' journey to Jerusalem under the weight of his passion, as well as his activity there (16:21—25:46). The confession by Peter at Caesarea Philippi, along with Jesus' promise for his church, is the midpoint and high point of the Gospel, shaped by Matthew in a different way from Mark's form, and has tremendous significance for the evangelist's purposes. . . . A second climax is then attained in the grand concluding scene (28:16–20). . . .

4. Time and Circumstances of the Composition: The Author

Matthew wrote after the **Jewish War** and the destruction of Jerusalem (22:7). The break with Judaism, which had become strong under the leadership of the Pharisaic scribes, had occurred (cf. 27:25; 10:17; 23:34). The tension with these circles who now lived according to strict interpretation of the law is discernible . . . , and the self-awareness of the church as the true "people of God" has been reinforced (21:43). Accordingly, the composition of this work is to be dated around A.D. 85–90. It may have been occasioned in part by the conflict with Judaism, to which the Jewish Christians living in the Christian community were still conscious of many ties; but a "crisis" is not evident. The danger of believers in Christ backsliding into the Jewish religion of the law, of Jewish Christianity divorcing itself from the church (as is testified for the second century A.D.), is not acute.

> **The Jewish War** A major revolt of Jerusalem against Rome (ca. AD 66–70) that resulted in the Romans' destruction of the city and the Jewish Temple.

Instead, Matthew seeks to proclaim the fulfillment of Israel's messianic expectations in Jesus Christ ("fulfillment quotations"), the superiority of the gospel to the religion of the Torah (5:17–48), and the constitution of a new community of salvation of both Jews and non-Jews, so

> 66 *Matthew seeks to proclaim the fulfillment of Israel's messianic expectations in Jesus Christ.* 99

as to establish all believers in Christ in the church of Jesus Christ (16:18). This church, which Matthew vividly portrays in their situation in the local community, is his primary concern. That church must produce the expected fruits (7:16–20; 12:33; 21:43). A strong pastoral and missionary aim outweighs polemics and apologetics.

But since the community could gain self-understanding and live out its life only from an assimilation of the proclamation and activity of Jesus the Messiah, Matthew sought to gather all the traditions of the person and work, passion and resurrection, of Jesus Christ into a single document and offer them to his community in an easy-to-grasp form corresponding to its life. To what extent the Christians sought to promote the influence of this Gospel beyond the local area, on other communities of the larger church, is uncertain. Indeed, the Gospel's effect was great, and it became the preferred Gospel of the entire church. . . .

According to early church tradition based on Papias (around A.D. 130), the author is the apostle Matthew, who is seen in the Gospel itself as the "tax collector" of 10:3. This tax collector, however, who held a banquet for Jesus and his disciples, is called "Levi" in Mark 2:14 (and Luke 5:27), and only the author of Matthew has identified the otherwise unknown Levi with the apostle. This explains the ancient Christian tradition, but without adequate grounds. Nor is the supposition of a "pre-Matthean" Gospel, inferred from the testimony of the Papias text, tenable. The Gospel of Matthew is an original Greek work, and the evangelist may have been a second-generation (Hellenistic) Jew. The frequent view, often represented in more recent scholarship, that Matthew

Hellenistic Jew A Jew who was raised in ancient Greek and Roman cultures, learning the Greek language and customs along with their Jewish faith.

was not a Jew by birth but a Gentile Christian, is scarcely justifiable. He writes for a community that embraces both groups; but he is best regarded as a person with Jewish views and Jewish ways of speaking.

For Reflection

1. Explain the differences between the beginnings and endings of Matthew's Gospel and Mark's Gospel. What was the author of Matthew's Gospel seeking to convey with these differences?

2. Which tensions in the community for which he wrote did the author of Matthew's Gospel seek to address and alleviate?

3. Read the following three verses from Matthew's Gospel cited in the reading, concerning the need for the Church to "produce the expected fruits": 7:16–20, 12:33, 21:43. What message did the author of Matthew's Gospel deliver in these passages, in light of the tensions in the community for which he wrote?

24 The Gospel of Mark

Introduction

"Who do you say that I am?" This question, which Jesus poses to his disciples at the turning point of Mark's Gospel (Mark 8:29), serves as the Gospel's central focus. An understanding of who Jesus is—the Messiah and Son of God—is complete only when his identity and mission are reconciled. Through Jesus' life we learn what being a disciple means, and through his death and Resurrection we are saved. God's favored Son must suffer and die for the salvation of all.

Mark's Gospel is the briefest, and likely earliest, of the four Gospels, believed to have been written around AD 70. Debate surrounds the identity of the author and place of writing, but the intended audience appears to have been a Christian group that was undergoing persecution. Rome is often suggested as the location because Emperor Nero's violent persecution around the years 62–64 would fit well within that timeline.

Mark's Gospel moves at a breathless pace. The word *immediately* is used dozens of times to describe Jesus' actions and journeys. To engage Mark's theology completely, one needs to recognize that Mark did not write a biography, catechism, or systematic reflection on faith. Rather, he wrote a narrative preaching about Jesus, and so his theology of who Christ is and what following him (discipleship) entails is best understood within the context of the Gospel's plot and storyline.

The reading that follows comes from the New Testament scholar Pheme Perkins. The selection outlines the historical situation of the author of Mark's Gospel and the audience for which the Gospel was originally written. The reading also identifies essential truths about Christ, discipleship, and suffering that are present in Mark's Gospel. Together, these points help the modern reader understand the theological message of Mark's Gospel.

Excerpt from *Reading the New Testament*
By Pheme Perkins

The Composition of Mark

Mark begins with the words, "The beginning of the gospel of Jesus Christ, Son of God" (1:1). "Gospel" does not mean "book" here either. Mark 1:14–15 uses "gospel" for Jesus' preaching that the reign of God is at hand. That usage reminds us of the OT use of "gospel" for the announcement that God is coming to free the people. (Luke 4:18–19 has Jesus begin his ministry with the words of Is 61:1–2.) The sayings about suffering for "Jesus' sake and for the sake of the gospel" (Mark 8:35; 10:29) link Jesus and the preaching about him (also 13:10; 14:9). Mark's opening, then, would not have led its readers to expect a reporter's biography about Jesus. They would expect preaching about Jesus as Son of God.

Look at Mark 14:9. It suggests something more is meant by "gospel" than just repeating stories and sayings. By promising that a particular woman's action will be remembered wherever the gospel is preached, it makes us think of the story of Jesus as something larger into which the sayings and stories about Jesus fit. Scholars think that some of the individual stories may have been gathered into collections. The parables which form the basis for Jesus' teaching in Mark 4:1–34 might be taken from such a collection. The doubling of several miracle stories (calming the storm: Mk 4:35–41; 6:45–52; feeding the multitude: 6:34–44; 8:1–9; healing the blind: 8:22–26; 10:46–52) suggests that there may have even been different collections that contained different versions of the same story. The story of Jesus' passion which we find in Mark 14–15 is probably based on an earlier written account of these events. While scholars can agree that Mark has probably used written sources as well as oral traditions about Jesus, it is much more difficult to move from the text of Mark as we have it back to the wording of a "pre-Markan" source.

As far as we know, Mark was the first person to bring the diverse stories about Jesus together in a single narrative. Mark writes in Greek for an audience that does not understand the **Aramaic** words which occur in some of the stories (5:41; 7:34; 15:34). They are also unfamiliar with Jewish customs (7:3–4). Mark 7:31 suggests that the author of the gospel was not familiar with Palestinian geography. (Try tracing the proposed route on a map!) Mark 13:2 suggests that the fall of Jerusalem to the Roman army has either occurred or will soon. The warnings against false messiahs and the command to flee (Mk 13:5–7,14–16,21–22) could be directed against expectations about the return of Jesus that had been awakened by those events. Mark has edited together these prophetic sayings with what appears to be an address to the situation of the readers in 13:9–13. They must expect to suffer for Jesus' sake at the hands of all the political authorities in the world: synagogue officials, Roman governors and even kings. This suffering is linked with the preaching of the gospel throughout the world. Mark 14:9 also referred to the gospel being preached "in the whole cosmos."

Church tradition later linked the author of the gospel with the Mark who is said to have been with Peter during his imprisonment in Rome (1 Pet 5:13). We also find a Mark associated with Paul's imprisonment there (2 Tim 4:11; Col 4:10). That tradition assumed that the references to suffering were to Nero's persecution. Another old tradition held that a "Mark" had founded the church in Alexandria. Citations from a gospel claiming to be a "secret version" of Mark preserved in Alexandria appear in a letter that is said to be by the third century teacher Clement of

> ### The Author of Mark's Gospel
>
> Mark's Gospel is traditionally attributed to a Jewish Christian believed to be a disciple of Peter named John Mark. The Gospel was written around AD 70, most likely near Rome, for an audience of non-Jewish Christians who were being persecuted for their belief in Jesus. The author of Mark's Gospel sought to teach about the identity of Jesus and discipleship to Christians being persecuted at the hands of the Roman Empire.

Aramaic A Semitic language similar to Hebrew that Palestinian Jews spoke at the time of Jesus.

Alexandria. Some modern scholars think that the concern with the destruction of the Jerusalem temple and the theme of Jesus' kingship which appear in the final chapters of the gospel points to origins in the region of Syro-Palestine. As followers of Jesus who did not join the Jews in revolt, Christians would have suffered at the hands of both parties. To Jewish nationalists, they are traitors. To Roman officials and the Gentile inhabitants of the region, they are "Jewish sympathizers." Perhaps the promise that the disciples would see the risen Lord in Galilee (Mk 14:28; 16:7) was even addressed to the community's own flight from the hostilities.

Whatever the circumstances in which Mark was written, the gospel's composition leaves little doubt that the truth of Jesus is only found on the cross. The center of the plot comes with Peter's confession that Jesus is messiah, the passion prediction and the rebuke of Peter (Mark 8:27–33). Christians are told that they too must be prepared to suffer (8:34–38).

As you read through Mark you will notice that the story is broken up into small units that often begin and end abruptly. You will find other passages in which Mark has apparently provided a generalized summary to fill in between two episodes (see 1:21–22 which fills in between the call of the disciples and the first exorcism which attracts attention to Jesus). One of Mark's favorite methods of composition is to fit two stories together by putting one in the middle of the other. In Mk 2:1–12 and 3:1–6, miracles of healing have sayings about Jesus' authority to forgive and the appropriateness of healing on the sabbath inserted in the middle. The story of the withered fig tree forms the outside framework for Jesus' cleansing of the temple in Mk 11:12–25. The healing of Jarius' [sic] daughter is interrupted by the healing of a woman who had been hemorrhaging for twelve years (Mk 5:21–43). Both of these stories emphasize the faith of the persons who ask Jesus for healing. The mission of the twelve disciples frames the story of John the Baptist's death (Mk 6:6–30).

The biggest puzzles in Mark center on what is called the **"messianic secret."** Even though Jesus is Son of God and a powerful teacher and healer, he sometimes commands

messianic secret A theme in the Gospel of Mark in which the disciples and others are shown as recognizing Jesus' identity as the Messiah but are instructed by Jesus not to tell anyone else.

people to remain silent. This theme leads to a story of a leper in 1:40–45 immediately disobeying Jesus by telling everyone. The disciples are also commanded to keep silent about the transfiguration (Mk 9:9). Even Jesus' teaching seems to be somewhat of a riddle, which even his disciples have a hard time understanding (Mk 4:10–13). The key to this puzzle lies in the middle of the gospel. Peter recognizes that Jesus is God's messiah and is immediately told not to tell anyone (8:27–30). The reason for the silence must be connected with what follows. Jesus tries to explain to his disciples that his role as messiah is one of suffering and death (8:31–33). The "messianic secret" points to the paradox of who Jesus is: the powerful Son of God who is destined to die on the cross. . . .

Summary

Mark's gospel paints a powerful picture of Jesus as the suffering Son of Man. We see the divine authority of Jesus in both miraculous deeds and in teaching. We see a full range of human reactions to Jesus, from the extravagant love of the woman who anoints him before his passion to the fears of his disciples and the mocking hostility of religious and political authorities. Since Jesus has power to break up Satan's empire and to control natural phenomena, we cannot agree with the crowd that he failed to save himself from the cross because he was unable to do so. Instead, we are forced to accept the death of Jesus as part of God's plan for the salvation of humanity.

That insight about the cross is so central to Mark that it shapes the whole gospel. It also shapes Mark's vision of discipleship. For Mark the concrete issues of Christian life are very few. They are summarized in love of God and neighbor and the willingness to follow Jesus' example of self-sacrificing service. No persons are excluded

> *" Mark's gospel paints a powerful picture of Jesus as the suffering Son of Man. "*

from God's love and forgiveness. No one can claim that being a disciple of the suffering Son of Man gives him or her a position of superiority over others. No one should be so naive as to think that the life of discipleship will be without failures and setbacks. But whatever the difficulties and confusion, whatever the cost in personal or material terms, Mark insists that Jesus is there "ahead of his disciples," always reaching out to save them.

For Reflection

1. Based on the information in the reading, explain the meaning of the word *Gospel* as it is used at the beginning of Mark's Gospel.

2. How does understanding the situation of the persecuted audience inform our understanding of the message of Mark's Gospel?

3. Explain what is meant by the term messianic secret and provide examples of how Mark presents this secret.

4. Summarize what the reading calls "the concrete issues of Christian life" presented in Mark's Gospel.

25 The Gospel of Luke

Introduction

Luke, a disciple and missionary coworker of the Apostle Paul, is the attributed author of both the Gospel of Luke and the Acts of the Apostles. In the introduction of his Gospel, he set out the reason he was writing it: "I too have decided, after investigating everything accurately anew, to write it down in an orderly sequence for you, most excellent **Theophilus,** so that you may realize the certainty of the teachings you have received" (Luke 1:3–4). Though others had written accounts of Jesus' life, Luke set out to write a more refined and orderly account following extensive research. It is believed that Luke used the Gospel of Mark and the "Q" source in the writing of his Gospel. Scholars also believe that he used another source unique to his Gospel.

Luke was writing for a largely Gentile audience that had entirely different needs from the audiences for Mark's or Matthew's Gospels. For many of Luke's readers, the region where Jesus preached was an unknown land. Additionally, they were unfamiliar with many of the Jewish writings referenced in Jesus' preaching. Luke was writing for a society where the poor were oppressed and the rich had special privileges. Luke's audience was facing questions such as, Do we have to become Jewish to become Christian? What should be our Christian attitude toward those who are poor and marginalized?

Theophilus In Greek *Theophilus* means "friend of God" or "lover of God." The Gospel of Luke and the Acts of the Apostles are addressed to Theophilus. The name may be that of a real person or an honorary title used to appeal to Greek-speaking Gentiles who believed in the God of Israel.

How can we ourselves follow Jesus in our lives? For this reason Luke's Gospel stresses certain themes, such as salvation for all, what it means to live as a Christian, and the love and mercy found in Christ. As the reading below states, the author of Luke "wanted his readers to know that they had been included in God's plan of salvation from the beginning."

This chapter's selection comes from a prominent and accessible commentary on Luke's Gospel by the Benedictine biblical scholar Jerome Kodell. The reading is useful for two reasons. First, it provides an overview of the audience and author of Luke's Gospel. Second, this reading outlines the major themes found throughout Luke's Gospel. Understanding both the audience and the themes of the Gospel, we are better able to understand and respond to the truths conveyed within its words.

Excerpt from *The Collegeville Bible Commentary: Luke*
By Jerome Kodell

Introduction

The Gospel of Luke is the first half of a two-part work that tells the story of the origins of Christianity from the infancy of Jesus until the arrival of Paul, the foremost preacher, in Rome around A.D. 60. Just the length of the Gospel and of its companion volume, the Acts of the Apostles (more extensive than the contribution of any other individual New Testament writer), would have made its author a prominent influence on Christian theology and spirituality. But he is in addition a gifted writer, organizing his materials creatively and telling his story with clarity and artistic coloring. Dante called Luke the "scribe of Christ's gentleness" because of his emphasis on Jesus' mercy to sinners and outcasts. Some of the most memorable Gospel stories of divine mercy are found only in Luke (the widow of Naim [*sic*], the prodigal son, Zacchaeus).

The Author and His Audience

At the beginning of his Gospel, Luke recognizes the work of those who have gone before. He is not trying to replace the earlier Gospel of Mark, but he sees the need for a new account for a new generation in different circumstances. Luke is a Greek-speaking Christian, possibly a convert of Paul, writing in Antioch (Syria) or Asia Minor (modern Turkey) late in the first century—probably in the eighties. The Christian church is quickly becoming more Gentile than Jewish in composition; it is no longer confined to Palestine but is a configuration of communities scattered throughout the Roman Empire. Its language is not Aramaic but Greek. Luke wants to show the continuity of this modern Greek church with Jesus and the early Hebrew community. He finds that he can trace these roots best by adding a sequel to the story of Jesus, connecting the two parts thematically while preserving the historical distinctions. He uses the Gospel of Mark, editing it according to his own needs, and other written and oral sources besides, some from traditions used also by the evangelist Matthew.

> ### The Author of Luke's Gospel
>
> The author of the Gospel of Luke was a Gentile Christian writing for Greek Gentile Christians around AD 80–90. Traditionally, Luke is thought to have been a disciple of Paul. Many scholars believe Luke might have traveled with Paul on one of his last mission journeys. Some of the stories from Paul's journeys are told in the first person in the Acts of the Apostles (for example, see Acts, chapter 21). Luke may have been one of Paul's most loyal disciples (see 2 Timothy 4:11).

To Luke's readership, the geography, language, and religious and political conditions of Palestine were foreign and remote. Most were unfamiliar with the Jewish writings that the preachers often referred to in explaining the story of Jesus. The Christians of Asia Minor and Europe were concerned to be good citizens of the Roman Empire, a government that had been treated as an intruder by many of Jesus' contemporaries in Palestine. Many of the new generation of Christians were not poor but well-to-do, more urban than rural. The question arose, either spontaneously or with help from their pagan neighbors: Why are we Greeks following a religion with so much of a Hebrew core? How did the news about Jesus get here? Were our missionaries reliable? Are we by now independent of happenings in Jerusalem?

These Christian citizens of the Roman Empire would have heard, of course, of the destruction of Jerusalem by the Roman army, a catastrophe foretold by Jesus and interpreted as punishment for sin. Did this indicate that they should cut their Jewish roots? How could Jesus' words to a Hebrew audience a half century earlier be appropriate to a modern Greek audience? All this would have been heightened by their neighbors' pervasive hostility to Christianity and by subtle persecution in many forms, particularly social and economic.

Issues like these swirled about Luke as he conceived his two-part work. He addressed these and more, directly and indirectly. He wanted his readers to know that they had been included in God's plan of salvation from the beginning, even though historically the Jews were the first to hear the message as the channel for all others. The story of salvation unraveled according to the exact plan of God, just as was promised in the Old Testament. It is a journey to the kingdom under the guidance of the Holy Spirit. The Gospel portrays the beginnings of the Christian story, from the first announcement of the fulfillment of salvation until its achievement in the death and resurrection of Jesus. The Acts of the Apostles tells of the rise and development of the church, pointing out the major decisions and turning points as the leaders were guided by God into the Gentile mission. Once the church's decision to evangelize all people, not only Jews, is made definitively (Acts 15), the story follows the apostle Paul as he carries the gospel across the Empire, into Europe and eventually to the center of the contemporary world, Rome.

Themes

Every preacher of the gospel delivers the fundamental proclamation of salvation in Jesus Christ. But each one develops the insights into the mystery that come from personal reflection and experience and that are needed by a particular audience. There are four written Gospels; there might have been many more. They tell us the same basic story about Jesus and interpret its meaning. Their approach to the subject is like that of four painters assigned to produce portraits of the same person. Each evangelist brings to the task a personal relationship to Jesus, individual talents, a particular experience of Christian life in a certain place or places, a wealth of material learned in the community or researched in other ways. Some of Luke's prominent themes are the following.

1. Salvation for all. The realization that God wants to save all people goes back to the earliest times in Israel's life as a people (Gen 13:2). All the communities of the earth would find blessing through the Hebrews. The early Jewish Christians knew this well, but they had to struggle with the question: Does God mean to open up salvation in Jesus to everyone directly, or should we bring converts in through Judaism? The decision had already been made in favor of universal salvation by the time any of the Gospels

> ❝ *Luke is determined to make the teaching of Jesus applicable to his readers living a middle-class life in a cosmopolitan society.* ❞

were written, so this theme is present beginning with the earliest, the Gospel of Mark. But reflection on this truth proceeded in various directions. Luke seems to have the most thoroughgoing message of universal salvation. Matthew's Gospel, for example, has the mandate to preach to all nations (Matt 28:19), but Jewish rejection of Jesus still smolders (Matt 27:25). Luke is not affected by this kind of anguish, and he stresses that Jesus is still available for Jews who turn to him (Acts 3:17–20).

2. Mercy and forgiveness. This theme has already been pointed out as distinctive of Luke's portrait of Jesus. In this Gospel, Jesus is constantly concerned to help the poor, the sinner, the outcast. Shepherds instead of Magi come to his crib (2:8–18); he welcomes the sinful but penitent woman at a Pharisee's meal (7:36–50); he speaks well of Samaritans (10:30–37); he seeks hospitality from a tax collector (19:1–10). The place of women in Luke's Gospel is also noteworthy in this regard. Women were second-class, often mistreated citizens of the world at that time. Jesus befriended women (10:38–42) and accepted their help (8:1–3); they did not weaken in faithfulness at the time of his passion and death (23:49; 24:1; Acts 1:14).

3. Joy. Luke's Gospel radiates the joy of salvation. The joy flows from a confidence in God's love and mercy as demonstrated in the teaching and action of Jesus described in the previous section. The births of John the Baptist and Jesus are announced as causes of great joy (1:14; 2:10). The repentance of a sinner is a source of great joy in heaven (15:7–10). The Gospel ends with the disciples returning to Jerusalem full of joy after Jesus' ascension (24:52).

> 66 **Luke's Gospel radiates the joy of salvation.** 99

4. The journey. All three synoptic Gospels (Matthew, Mark, Luke) begin the account of Jesus' public ministry with John's preaching from Isaiah: "Make ready the way of the Lord, clear him a straight path" (Isa 40:3). The mission of Jesus is presented as the continuation and culmination of the "way of the Lord" that began when Abraham left his homeland, and continued with the Exodus from Egypt led by Moses and, later, the return from the **Babylonian captivity.** Luke capitalizes on the journey theme to organize the central section of his Gospel (9:51—19:44) around the final journey of Jesus from Galilee to Jerusalem.

The Father's guidance of Jesus and the church brings to the fore emphases on the role of the Holy Spirit and the place of prayer. Luke is occasionally referred to as the "Evangelist of the Holy Spirit" or the "Evangelist of Prayer." The role of the Spirit begins before Jesus' birth (1:35, 67). Jesus is led by the Spirit into the desert (4:1) and on returning announces that he is the one foretold on whom the Spirit rests (4:18). This theme continues even more strongly in the Acts of the Apostles as the Spirit empowers the disciples to preach the gospel (Acts 2:1–17). The Spirit guides the emerging church in deciding how to expand the mission (15:28) and leads the missionaries on their journeys (16:6–7). Prayer is the context for the opening announcement of salvation (Luke 1:10). Jesus prays before choosing the Twelve (6:12); he is praying as he is about to be transfigured

Babylonian captivity Also referred to as the Exile (ca. 587–500 BC), when the Babylonians took a number of high-ranking Judeans into captivity in Babylon following the destruction of Jerusalem and the first Temple.

(9:29) and when the disciples ask him to teach them to pray (11:1). Prayer characterizes the community in Acts (Acts 1:24; 2:42; 3:1).

5. *Modern Christian living.* Luke is determined to make the teaching of Jesus applicable to his readers living a middle-class life in a cosmopolitan society. He indicates that good citizenship is compatible (and expected) with Christianity. This is more evident in Acts than in Luke's Gospel. Paul's Roman citizenship is carefully noted (Acts 16:37–40; 22:26), and his honorable civic conduct is insisted on (18:14–16). But already in the Gospel, Jesus is presented as an observant citizen maligned by false charges (Luke 20:25; 23:2). His death was at the hands of the Roman magistrate, true, but one who was too weak to free Jesus as he was convinced he should (23:1–25). If these good citizens were persecuted—the implication might further be—don't be alarmed at your own mistreatment in the cause of Christ.

The question of possessions is treated often. In Luke, Jesus' beatitudes are harsh and stark: "Blest are you poor. . . . Woe to you rich" (6:20, 24), but overall there is no simplistic message of personal despoilment. The point is rather that one must not be enslaved by attachment to possessions (12:13–43; 14:25–33); they must be expended on others (18:22). Renunciation extends even to one's personal relationships. Not even one's own family must come between the disciple and Jesus (14:26).

6. *Fulfillment of prophecy.* Jesus' mission of salvation had been prepared from ages past. Luke incorporates a surprising amount of Old Testament teaching for his Greek readers, though not as much as Matthew does. One of Luke's favorite usages is "it must happen"—"it had to happen" (2:49; 4:43; 9:22). The cross, the way of suffering, was a puzzle to his Greek readers—how revolting that the Savior, Son of God and King, should be treated so shamefully. Luke repeats again and again that the suffering had to be: it is the way to glory (18:31–33; 24:26).

7. *Ascension.* Luke sees the goal of Jesus' mission as "to be taken (up) from this world" (9:51; 24:51). The ascension comes in the event of the resurrection; it is the act of glorification whereby Jesus takes his place at the right hand of the Father. The ascension is crucial to Jesus' saving work, because it is through this glorification that the Spirit is released on the church (Acts 2:33) and salvation is made available for all people.

For Reflection

1. Why would it be important for the author of Luke's Gospel to recount for his particular audience Jesus' life from the moment of the announcement that he was to be born through his Ascension?

2. According to the chapter's reading, how did Luke's theme of salvation for all relate to the community for which he was writing?

3. Why is Luke called the "Evangelist of the Holy Spirit" and the "Evangelist of Prayer"?

4. The author of this reading describes Luke's lessons for a "modern," or cosmopolitan Greek Christian, audience. How are his teachings applicable today?

26 The Gospel of John

Introduction

The Gospel of John is often described as offering a "mystical" portrayal of Jesus and his ministry. John differs widely from the other three synoptic Gospels. Unlike the synoptic Gospels, John does not begin with an infancy narrative or with Jesus' public ministry. Instead John's Gospel begins with the same words that begin the Book of Genesis: "In the beginning" (1:1). In the synoptic Gospels, Jesus' ministry lasts only a few months or a year (at most); he performs numerous miracles and often speaks in short parables or sayings. In John's account, however, Jesus' ministry lasts three years, he performs only seven signs to demonstrate the mystery of the Incarnation (Jesus becoming man while remaining fully divine), and he speaks in long monologues. In addition, John's Gospel has no Last Supper account.

The reasons for these differences between the synoptic Gospels and the Gospel of John have always puzzled scholars. Scholars once thought that John knew of the other Gospels but wished to develop a more mystical and symbolic explanation of Jesus' life instead of the historical rendering seen in the other three. Another school of thought is that the author of John's Gospel had no knowledge whatsoever of the synoptic Gospels and that the similarities between John and the synoptic Gospels was attributable to the oral tradition that began with the Apostles. Between these extremes is a belief, supported by the reading included in this chapter, that "Mark and John shared common preGospel traditions, oral or written" and that the author of John's Gospel "was familiar with traditions incorporated later into Luke" (Brown, *An Introduction to the New Testament,* page 365). Scholars today continue to debate this relationship among the Gospels—but almost all agree that the differences in the Gospel of John likely were affected by the peculiar circumstances of his community in Ephesus.

As mentioned previously, each Gospel author communicated his message for a specific audience. The community for which John's Gospel was written was struggling with being expelled from the Jewish synagogue because they emphasized Jesus' divinity. Later the community had to deal with a **schism,** or major division, because some members were emphasizing the divinity of Jesus to the exclusion of his humanity. Addressing these and other circumstances, John's Gospel strongly emphasizes the truth of the Incarnation as necessary for salvation.

Raymond Brown, one of the greatest Catholic biblical scholars of his generation, was a prominent commentator on the Gospel and letters of John. Below is a section from his *Introduction to the New Testament*. This reading is a concise, accessible explanation of the distinctions between John and the synoptic Gospels, as well as the history of the community in Ephesus and the **Johannine** writings.

schism A major break or separation.

Johannine An adjective used to describe something pertaining to John's Gospel, including the community, tradition, and letters.

Excerpt from *An Introduction to the New Testament*

By Raymond E. Brown

Comparison of John to the Synoptic Gospels

A comparison of the Fourth Gospel to the first three Gospels shows obvious differences. Peculiarities of John include: a Jesus conscious of having preexisted with God before he came into the world (John 17:5); a public ministry largely set in Jerusalem rather than in Galilee; the significant absence of the kingdom of God motif (only in 3:3,5); long discourses and dialogues rather than parables; no diabolic possessions; a very restricted number of miracles (seven?), including some that are unique (changing of water to wine at Cana, healing a man born blind, and the raising of Lazarus). According to statistics supplied by B. de Solages in a French study (1979) there are parallels to Mark in 15.5 percent of John's passion narrative; the parallels to Mark in the Matthean and Lucan passion narratives would be four times higher.

> **The Author of John's Gospel**
>
> Although the fourth Gospel is traditionally attributed to the Apostle John, the author of John's Gospel is unknown. Many scholars believe he was a member of a Christian community possibly founded by the Beloved Disciple. The Gospel is believed to have been written between AD 90 and 100 to address the needs of a Jewish Christian community that may have included Gentiles and Samaritans.

Yet there are also important similarities to the Synoptics, especially in the beginning narrative of the ministry featuring **JBap** and in the concluding narratives of the passion and empty tomb. In particular, the closest similarities are with Mark, e.g., in the sequence of events shared by John 6 and Mark 6:30–54; 8:11–33; and in such verbal details as "genuine nard of great value" (John 12:3), 300 **denarii** (12:5), and 200 denarii (6:7). There are parallels with Luke[1], but more of motif than of wording, e.g., figures like Martha and Mary, Lazarus (parabolic in Luke), and Annas; lack of a night trial before Caiaphas; the three "not guilty" statements in the Pilate trial; postresurrectional appearances of Jesus *in Jerusalem* to his male disciples; the miraculous draught of fishes (John 21). There are fewer similarities with Matthew; yet compare John 13:16 with Matt 10:24; and John 15:18–27 with Matt 10:18–25.

A variety of solutions has been suggested. At one end of the spectrum, some would posit John's knowledge of Mark or even

> **JBap** Scholarly shorthand for John the Baptist.
>
> **denarii** Plural of denarius, a form of money in the Roman Empire.

of all three Synoptics. (Such proposals may disagree as to whether John *also* had an independent tradition.) At the other end of the spectrum, the fourth evangelist is thought not to have known any Synoptic Gospel and occasional similarities between John and the others are explained in terms of the Synoptic and Johannine Traditions independently reproducing with variations the same deeds or sayings. In between the extremes a median position (that I espouse myself) maintains that Mark and John shared common preGospel traditions, oral or written; and that although the fourth evangelist had not seen the final form of Luke, he was familiar with traditions incorporated later into Luke. Some who make a distinction in John between an evangelist and a final redactor would posit that only the latter knew one or more of the Synoptic Gospels. . . .

History of the Johannine Community

As noted in discussing the Synoptic Gospels, because the Jesus material was shaped by each evangelist for an intended audience, indirectly the Gospels may give us theological and sociological information about the Christians who preserved, shaped, and/or received the memories of him. John's Gospel presentation of Jesus is strongly characterized by debates and adversarial situations, and we have three Epistles of John clearly echoing Johannine thought but more openly addressed to an audience and its problems. Consequently it may be that one can reconstruct more of the background of John than that of any other Gospel. Yet one should not confuse such reconstructive research with exegesis, which has to do with what the Gospel meant

> " *John's Gospel presentation of Jesus is strongly characterized by debates and adversarial situations.* "

to convey to its readers. The evangelist tells us his purpose in 20:31, and it was not to recount background.

I shall now present a reconstruction of the community history, warning that while it explains many factors in the Gospel, it remains a hypothesis and "perhaps" needs to be added to every sentence. The reconstruction covers not only the Gospel and its redaction but also the Johannine Epistles. . . . Four phases are involved. (1) A phase preceding the written

Gospel but shaping its thought (up to the 70s or 80s). In or near Palestine, Jews of relatively standard expectations, including followers of JBap, accepted Jesus as the **Davidic Messiah,** the fulfiller of the prophecies, and one confirmed by miracles (see the titles in John 1). Among them, insignificantly at first, was a man who had known Jesus and become his disciple during the public ministry and who would become the Beloved Disciple. To these first followers were added Jews of an anti-Temple bias who made converts in Samaria (John 4). They understood Jesus primarily against a Mosaic background (as distinct from a Davidic one): Jesus had been with God, whom he had seen and whose word he brought down to this world. The acceptance of this second group catalyzed the development of a high, preexistence christology (seen against the background of divine Wisdom) that led to debates with Jews who thought that Johannine Christians were abandoning Jewish monotheism by making a second God out of Jesus (5:18). Ultimately the leaders of these Jews had Johannine Christians expelled from synagogues (9:22; 16:2). The latter, alienated from their own, turned very hostile to "the Jews," whom they regarded as children of the devil (8:44). They stressed a realization of the eschatological promises in Jesus to compensate for what they had lost in Judaism (whence the strong theme of replacement in the Gospel). At the same time the Johannine Christians despised believers in Jesus who did not make the same public break from the synagogue (exemplified by the parents of the blind man in 9:21–23; also 12:42–43). The disciple mentioned above made this transition and helped others to make it, thus becoming the Beloved Disciple.

(2) The phase during which the basic Gospel was written by the evangelist. Since "the Jews" were considered blind and unbelieving (12:37–40), the coming of the Greeks was seen as God's plan of fulfillment (12:20–23). The community or part of it may have moved from Palestine to the **diaspora** to teach the Greeks (7:35), perhaps to the Ephesus area—a move that would cast light

Davidic Messiah A Messiah who would stand in the line of King David as the rightful heir of the throne to rule over a renewed Kingdom of Israel.

on the Hellenistic atmosphere of the Gospel and on the need to explain Semitic names and titles (e.g., rabbi, Messiah). This context brought out universalist possibilities in Johannine thought, in an attempt to speak to a wider audience. Rejection and persecution, however, convinced Johannine Christians that the world (like "the Jews") was opposed to Jesus. They looked on themselves as not of this world which was under the power of Satan, the Prince of this world (17:15–16; 14:30; 16:33). In their relation to other Christians, they rejected some as having so inadequate a christology that they were really unbelievers (6:60–66). Others symbolized by Simon Peter truly believed in Jesus (6:67–69) but were not deemed so perceptive as the Johannine Christians symbolized by the Beloved Disciple (20:6–9). The hope was that the divisions between them and the Johannine community might be healed and they might be one (10:16; 17:11). However, the Gospel's one-sided emphasis on the divinity of Jesus (shaped by struggles with the synagogue leaders) and on the need for love of one another as the sole commandment (13:34; 15:12,17) opened the way for some in the next generation whose whole knowledge of Jesus came from that Gospel to develop exaggerated views.

(3) The phase during which the Johannine Epistles, I and II John, were written (ca. AD 100). The community split in two: (a) Some adhered to the view represented by the author of I and II John (another Johannine writer distinct from the evangelist). He complemented the Gospel by stressing the humanity of Jesus (come in the flesh) and ethical behavior (keeping the commandments); (b) Many seceded (at least, in the view of the author of I John 2:18–19) and were antichrists and children of the devil because they had so exaggerated Jesus' divinity that they did not see any importance in his human career or in their own behavior (beyond simply believing in Jesus). Yet in the Johannine community there was no

diaspora Refers to a community of people who live in exile from their native land. In the Old Testament, the Diaspora of the Jewish people began in 587 BC, when the Temple in Jerusalem was destroyed and many Jews were taken into captivity in Babylon.

structure sufficiently authoritative to enable the author to discipline the secessionists who were actively seeking more adherents; he could only urge those who were puzzled about truth to test the Spirits (I John 4:1–6).

(4) The phase during which III John was written and the redactor added chap. 21 (AD 100–110?). The disintegration of the Johannine community led to a development of pastoral structure and brought those sympathetic to the christology described under 3a closer to the larger "church catholic." In III John, even though the writer did not like him because he had become authoritative, Diotrephes probably represented this new trend which was alien to the preceding Johannine reliance on the Spirit alone as teacher. Similarly in John 21:15–17 Jesus gives Simon Peter the task of feeding the sheep and thus recognizes human pastors alongside Jesus, the model shepherd. This development would ultimately bring some Johannine Christians into the larger church and preserve the Johannine heritage for that church.

Endnotes

1. J.A. Bailey, *The Traditions Common to the Gospels of Luke and John* (NovTSup 7; Leiden: Brill, 1963); F.L. Cribbs, SBLSP 1978, 1.215–61.

For Reflection

1.   What differences and similarities between John's Gospel and the synoptic Gospels does Raymond Brown identify?

2.   The author states that "the evangelist tells us his purpose in 20:31, and it was not to recount background." Read John 20:31 and summarize in your own words the stated purpose for writing the Gospel.

3.   What challenges were present in the first phase of the Johannine community's history, as recounted by the author?

For Further Reading

Barton, John, and John Muddiman (ed.). *The Oxford Bible Commentary*. New York: Oxford University Press, 2001.

Binz, Stephen. *Introduction to the Bible: A Catholic Guide to Studying Scripture*. Collegeville, MN: The Liturgical Press, 2007.

Brown, Raymond E. *An Introduction to the New Testament*. New York: Doubleday, 1997.

Carvalho, Corrine. *Encountering Ancient Voices: A Guide to Reading the Old Testament*. Winona, MN: Anselm Academic, 2010.

Cassian, John. (Edgar C. S. Gibson, transl.) "The Conferences of John Cassian." In *A Select Library of Nicene and Post-Nicene Fathers of the Christian Church*. New York, 1894. At *www.ccel.org/ccel/cassian/conferences.i.html*.

Catechism of the Catholic Church. Vatican City: Libreria Editrice Vaticana, 1997.

Collegeville Bible Commentary, The. Collegeville, MN: The Liturgical Press, 1989.

Dulles, Avery. *Revelation Theology: A History*. New York: Herder and Herder,1969.

Freedman, David Noel (ed.). *The Anchor Bible Dictionary*. New York: Doubleday, 1992.

Freedman, David Noel (ed.). *Eerdmans Dictionary of the Bible*. Grand Rapids, MI: Eerdmans, 2000.

Frigge, Marielle. *Beginning Biblical Studies*. Winona, MN: Anselm Academic, 2009.

Halbur, Virginia, and Brian Singer-Towns (eds.). *Understanding the Bible: A Guide to Reading the Scriptures*. Winona, MN: Saint Mary's Press, 2008.

Howard, Evan B. *The Brazos Introduction to Christian Spirituality*. Grand Rapids, MI: Brazos, 1991.

John Paul II, Pope. *Faith and Reason (Fides et Ratio)*, 1998. At *www.vatican.vaedocs/ENG0216/_INDEX.HTM*.

John Paul II, Pope. *Splendor of Truth, The (Veritatis Splendor,* 1993). At *www.vatican.va/edocs/ENG0222/_INDEX.HTM*.

Matthews, Victor. *Manners and Customs in the Bible: An Illustrated Guide to Daily Life in Bible Times*. 3rd edition. Peabody, MA: Hendrickson, 2006.

McGrath, Alister E. (ed.). *The Christian Theology Reader*. 3rd edition. Malden, MA: Blackwell, 2007.

McKenzie, John. *Dictionary of the Bible*. New York: Simon and Schuster, 1965.

New Jerome Biblical Commentary, The. Englewood Cliffs, NJ: Prentice Hall, 1990.

Perkins, Pheme. *Reading the New Testament: An Introduction*. New York: Paulist Press, 1988.

Pius XII, Pope. *Divino Afflante Spiritu* (1943). At *www.vatican.va/holy_father/ pius_xii/encyclicals/documents/hf_p-xii_enc_30091943_divino-afflante- spiritu_en.html.*

Pontifical Biblical Commission. *The Jewish People and Their Sacred Scriptures in the Christian Bible*. Vatican City: Pontifical Biblical Commission, 2001. At *www.vatican.va/roman_curia/congregations/cfaith/pcb_documents/rc_con_cfaith_ doc_20020212_popolo-ebraico_en.html.*

Ratzinger, Joseph. *Introduction to Christianity*. San Francisco: Ignatius Press, 1990.

Ratzinger, Joseph. *Jesus of Nazareth*. New York: Doubleday, 2007.

Saint Mary's Press® College Study Bible. Winona, MN: Saint Mary's Press, 2006.

Schnackenburg, Rudolf. *The Gospel of Matthew*. Grand Rapids, MI: Eerdmans, 2002.

Scholz, Daniel J. *Jesus in the Gospels and Acts: Introducing the New Testament*. Winona, MN: Saint Mary's Press, 2009.

Second Vatican Council. *Dogmatic Constitution on Divine Revelation* (*Dei Verbum*, 1965). At *www.vatican.va/archive/hist_councils/ii_vatican_council/documents/ vat-ii_const_19651118_dei-verbum_en.html.*

Singer-Towns, Brian. *Biblical Literacy Made Easy: A Practical Guide for Catechists, Teachers, and Youth Ministers*. Winona, MN: Saint Mary's Press, 2008.

United States Conference of Catholic Bishops. *United States Catholic Catechism for Adults*. Washington, D.C.: United States Conference of Catholic Bishops, 2006.

Acknowledgments

The scriptural quotations on pages 66 and 145 are from the *New American Bible with Revised New Testament and Revised Psalms*. Copyright © 1991, 1986, and 1970 by the Confraternity of Christian Doctrine, Washington, D.C. Used by the permission of the copyright owner. All Rights Reserved. No part of the *New American Bible* may be reproduced in any form without permission in writing from the copyright owner.

The excerpts on pages 12–17, 61–65, and 86–89, the definition of *relativism* on page 24, and the quotation on page 61 are from the *United States Catholic Catechism for Adults*, by the United States Conference of Catholic Bishops (USCCB) (Washington, DC: USCCB, 2006), pages 525, 61, 12–15, 23–26, 26–27, 55–56, 57–60, and 27–31, respectively. Copyright © 2006 by the USCCB, Washington, D.C. All rights reserved. No part of this work may be reproduced or transmitted in any form or by any means, electronic or mechanical, including photocopying, recording, or by an information storage and retrieval system, without permission in writing from the copyright holder. Used with permission of the USCCB.

The excerpts on pages 19–22, 67–71, and 92–94 and the quotation on page 91 are from *Dogmatic Constitution on Divine Revelation* (*Dei Verbum*, 1965), numbers 1, 2, 3, 4, 5, 6, 7–10, 21–23, 11, 12, 13, and 11, respectively, at *www.vatican.va/archive/hist_councils/ii_vatican_council/documents/vat-ii_const_19651118_dei-verbum_en.html*. Copyright © Liberia Editrice Vaticana (LEV). Used with permission of LEV.

The quotation on page 24 and the excerpt on pages 25–28 are from *The Splendor of Truth (Veritatis Splendor),* numbers 5 and 1–3, at *www.vatican.va/holy_father/john_paul_ii/encyclicals/documents/hf_jp-ii_enc_06081993_veritatis-splendor_en.html*. Copyright © Liberia Editrice Vaticana (LEV). Used with permission of LEV.

The excerpts on pages 30–33 and 55–57 are reprinted from *The Christian Theology Reader*, third edition, edited by Alister E. McGrath (Oxford: Blackwell Publishing, 2007), pages 15–18 and 88–89. Copyright © 1996, 2001, 2007 by Alister E. McGrath. Used with permission of Blackwell Publishing, Ltd.

The excerpt on pages 37–39 is from *Introduction to Christianity*, by Joseph Cardinal Ratzinger, translated by J. R. Foster (San Francisco: Ignatius Press, 2004), pages 79–81. Revisions to the English edition and Preface copyright © 1990, 2004 Ignatius Press, San Francisco. Used with permission of Ignatius Press.

During this book's preparation, all citations, facts, figures, names, addresses, telephone numbers, Internet URLs, and other pieces of information cited within were verified for accuracy. The authors and Saint Mary's Press staff have made every attempt to reference current and valid sources, but we cannot guarantee the content of any source, and we are not responsible for any changes that may have occurred since our verification. If you find an error in, or have a question or concern about, any of the information or sources listed within, please contact Saint Mary's Press.